The New
Enchantment of America
MISSOURI

By Allan Carpenter

CHILDRENS PRESS, CHICAGO

ACKNOWLEDGMENTS

For assistance in the preparation of the revised edition, the author thanks:
DEAN BROOKS, Media Coordinator, Missouri Division of Tourism.

American Airlines—Anne Vitaliano, Director of Public Relations; *Capitol Historical Society,* Washington, D. C.; *Newberry Library,* Chicago, Dr. Lawrence Towner, Director; *Northwestern University Library,* Evanston, Illinois; *United Airlines*—John P. Grember, Manager of Special Promotions; Joseph P. Hopkins, Manager, News Bureau.

UNITED STATES GOVERNMENT AGENCIES: *Department of Agriculture*—Robert Hailstock, Jr., Photography Division, Office of Communication; Donald C. Schuhart, Information Division, Soil Conservation Service. *Army*—Doran Topolosky, Public Affairs Office, Chief of Engineers, Corps of Engineers. *Department of Interior*—Louis Churchville, Director of Communications; EROS Space Program—Phillis Wiepking, Community Affairs; Charles Withington, Geologist; Mrs. Ruth Herbert, Information Specialist; Bureau of Reclamation; National Park Service—Fred Bell and the individual sites; Fish and Wildlife Service—Bob Hines, Public Affairs Office. *Library of Congress*—Dr. Alan Fern, Director of the Department of Research; Sara Wallace, Director of Publications; Dr. Walter W. Ristow, Chief, Geography and Map Division; Herbert Sandborn, Exhibits Officer. *National Archives*—Dr. James B. Rhoads, Archivist of the United States; Albert Meisel, Assistant Archivist for Educational Programs; David Eggenberger, Publications Director; Bill Leary, Still Picture Reference; James Moore, Audio-Visual Archives. *United States Postal Service*—Herb Harris, Stamps Division.

For assistance in the preparation of the first edition, the author thanks:
Consultant Richard S. Brownlee, Director, Secretary, State Historical Society of Missouri; Governor Warren E. Hearnes; Raymond Roberts, Director of Curriculum, State Department of Education, Division of Public Schools; Division of Commerce and Industrial Development, State of Missouri; Chamber of Commerce of Metropolitan Saint Louis; and Chamber of Commerce, Kansas City.

Illustrations on the preceding pages:
Cover photograph: Jefferson National Expansion Memorial, St. Louis, James R. Rowan
Page 1: Commemorative stamps of historic interest
Pages 2-3: Fall in the mountains, Missouri Division of Tourism
Page 3: (Map) USDI Geological Survey
Pages 4-5: St. Louis Area, EROS Space Photo, USDI Geological Survey, EROS Data Center

Project Editor, Revised Edition:
   Joan Downing
Assistant Editor, Revised Edition:
   Mary Reidy

Library of Congress Cataloging in Publication Data
Carpenter, John Allan, 1917-
   Missouri.

   (His The new enchantment of America)
   SUMMARY: Describes the history, famous citizens, and places of interest of the "Show Me" state.

   1. Missouri—Juvenile literature.
   [1. Missouri] I. Title. II. Series: Carpenter, John Allan, 1917-   The new enchantment of America.
F466.3.C3   1978   977.8   78-3551
ISBN 0-516-04125-8

Contents

Laclede's settlement was already over 75 years old and a flourishing community when German artist Lewis painted it for his now rare book, Das Illustrirte Mississippithal, *published in color in Germany.*

A True Story to Set the Scene

For five weary days, thirty men toiled up the Mississippi River, poling heavy boats and dragging them over the many sandbars. "At the end of the fifth day (March 14, 1764) the first boat had reached the mouth of the gully at the head of which were the marked trees. . . . On the morning of the next day I put the men to work. . . . They commenced the shed, which was built in a short time and the little cabins for the men were built in the vicinity."

This event was an important one in history—it represented the beginning of the great city of St. Louis.

It was made even more interesting, however, because of a most unusual circumstance. The leader of that difficult expedition—the person whose words are quoted above—the first builder of St. Louis—was a thirteen-and-a-half-year old boy, Auguste Chouteau.

It seems unlikely that the beginning of any other great city of the world ever was supervised by anyone so young. The account of these events and the people who took part in them is one of the most interesting of the many stories of enchantment of Missouri.

The central figure in the account was Pierre Laclède Liguest. His merchandising firm—Maxtent, Laclède and Company—had been given a monopoly in the fur trade in the upper Louisiana country. Laclède left New Orleans on August 3, 1763, to establish his first trading post. We have no accurate report of why he made the incredible choice of a thirteen-year-old boy to be his second in command. However, Laclède was a capable man and a good judge of character. We can assume, among other more personal reasons, that Laclède felt the youthful Chouteau had already proven that he deserved an important post.

The expedition was a sizeable one as it started up the river with many boats and a large party. Chouteau tells us that this party had brought considerable armament. They reached Sainte Genevieve, which was already a village in present-day Missouri, but Laclède did not think it was suitable for his headquarters. Going on, Laclède left his merchandise at Fort de Chartres in Illinois and went out to locate a suitable spot for his new trading post.

When they came to the place where St. Louis now stands, Chouteau wrote that Laclede "was delighted to see the situation. He did not hesitate a moment to form there the establishment that he proposed. After having examined all thoroughly, he fixed upon the place where he wished to form his settlement, marked with his own hand some trees (It is said the site was covered with a beautiful grove of walnut trees.) and said to Chouteau, 'You will come here as soon as navigation opens and will cause this place to be cleared in order to form our settlement after the plan that I shall give you.' "

During the winter at Fort de Chartres, Laclède persuaded many of the settlers there to join him when his new settlement was ready. He chose the thirty tough, able men, mostly mechanics, to do the beginning work and showed his continuing confidence in young Chouteau by placing him in charge of the first building expedition. Apparently this remarkable teenager won the respect of these older men, for everything went smoothly.

Chouteau described Laclède's precise instruction: "You will proceed and land at the place where we marked the trees; you will commence to have the place cleared and build a large shed to contain the provisions and the tools, and some small cabins to lodge the men." As we have seen, Chouteau rewarded his leader's confidence by doing exactly as he was instructed.

When Laclède arrived in the early part of April after the first buildings were built, Chouteau tells how he "fixed a plan of the village which he wished to found, and he named it Saint Louis." According to historian Walter Stevens, "The plan which Laclède drew for his settlement is the basis of the present map of St. Louis."

Laclède wanted to found an establishment suitable to his commerce; he said he "Intended to establish a settlement which might hereafter become one of the finest in America." This extraordinary prophecy was based on his knowledge that the site of the future city was a really exceptional one—high enough to avoid floods and at an extremely good location.

The enterprise and the new community prospered over the years. When Laclède died, Auguste Chouteau became administrator of his estate. As time passed, Chouteau achieved a position as the leading man of business and the wealthiest citizen of upper Louisiana. He was chairman of the first board of the town of St. Louis, president of the Bank of Missouri, prosperous merchant, head of extensive lead-mining operations, and owner of extensive land holdings. He died in St. Louis February 24, 1829.

However, as long as he lived Auguste Chouteau remembered that search for a site and the starting of St. Louis which he and Laclède carried on together—two remarkable men, one who had the vision instantly to select the location of a great city and who also had the unusual perception to select a boy, who at the age of thirteen could begin to bring the vision to reality.

*More than a billion years old, Elephant Rocks near Graniteville
rank among the unique examples of Missouri's varied geography.*

Lay of the Land

A miniature United States is the way one expert has described Missouri. It is the cotton fields and delta lands of the Deep South; it is the rolling, grassy plains of the West, and the rich agricultural land of the Midwest; it is the industrial centers of the East and the dairyland of the North; it is the mountains of the Ozarks.

One of the unique geographic distinctions of Missouri is the fact that it is one of two states with borders touching eight other states. These are: Iowa, Nebraska, Kansas, Oklahoma, Arkansas, Tennessee, Kentucky, and Illinois.

Missouri is nineteenth in size among the states, with a total area of 69,674 square miles (about 180,000 square kilometers), of which a 548 square mile (about 1,400 square kilometers) area is covered by inland water. The state is usually divided into four major areas: Glaciated Plains in the north, Western Plains, Ozark region of the south, and Southeastern Lowlands. In southeast Missouri is the famous heel, a narrow extension below the southern border of the rest of the state.

The lowest regions of Missouri are part of the vast area called the Mississippi embayment. Geologists say that the Gulf of Mexico once reached about as far north as the present junction of the Mississippi and Ohio rivers. All the land below that point is really the enormous delta of the Mississippi—built up over the years by rich silt brought down from lands above.

In ancient times most of present-day Missouri was buried beneath age-old seas again and again, only to rise once more. Sometimes mountain ranges raised their heights and then were worn away over the centuries. They too sometimes rose again, only to be worn off once more. Although the highest point in Missouri is only the 1,772 foot (about 540 meters) summit of Taum Sauk Mountain, much of Missouri appears to be rugged and mountainous. This is due largely to what is known as high local relief. The mountains rise abruptly from their bases to considerable height so that there is great contrast in elevation between a stream valley and a nearby bluff or hill. The ancient pre-Cambrian knobs in the St. Francois Mountains, part of the Ozarks in southeastern Missouri, soar as much as 800 feet (about 244 meters) above adjoining stream beds. This is the most rugged mountainous area of Missouri.

Oddly enough, the lowest point in the state, 230 feet (about 70 meters) above sea level, is also in the southeast near Cardwell on the St. Francis River.

It is likely that no state has more large caves and caverns than Missouri. Twenty-six of these are open to the public on a commercial basis. There are also a number of natural bridges, carved through the soft rock by flowing streams.

Only two of the four great glaciers reached as far as Missouri, extending over most of the northern part of the state. Since this was the extreme southern edge of the glaciers, their deposits of rock, sand, gravel, and fine top soil are all generally less than in more northerly regions.

Other remnants of ancient times in Missouri are the fossils of living things found there. Especially interesting are the skeletons of elephants as well as of mastodons found near Kimmswick.

LIVING WATERS

Missouri is dominated by great rivers. The 500 mile (about 805 kilometers) border marking the course of the Mississippi River along the state is the second longest of any state on that river. Only two states—Missouri and Iowa—are bordered by both the Mississippi and Missouri rivers. Missouri and South Dakota are the only states both bordered and cut through by the Missouri River.

Thomas Hart Benton described the Missouri River as being "a little too thick to swim in and not quite thick enough to walk on." That thickness is due to the tremendous amount of silt it carries. The great force and changeable nature of both the Missouri and Mississippi rivers cause many boundary problems. The rivers may cut through a narrow neck of land and leave a whole former channel entirely separated, or they may fill up with sand bars and pass around some other way.

The treacherous, shifting channel of the Missouri River is particularly apt to change suddenly, throwing an area that once was in one state into its neighbor. There is a sizeable oval of Missouri state land on the west bank of the Missouri River at St. Joseph. Near the Iowa border a small circle of Nebraska land stretches east of the river on the Missouri side. In 1857 the shifting Missouri left Weston several miles inland.

Where the two great rivers come together they appear to flow separately for some distance—the muddy waters of the Missouri on one side and the clearer waters of the Mississippi on the other. Finally the waters merge, and the Mississippi is never the same again.

The geological survey of the Department of the Interior lists the major rivers of Missouri as the White, Black, Osage, and St. Francis, in addition to the Mississippi and Missouri. A divide through Missouri separates the waters flowing into the White River system and the Missouri River system.

Other Missouri rivers are the Grand, Chariton, James, Big Piney, Pomme de Terre, Meramec, Gasconade, Niangua, Cuivre, Marais des Cygnes (Marsh of the Swans), Big Tarkio, and Current. The Jacks Fork River is said to flow through the most nearly natural wilderness south of Minnesota and east of the Rockies. Picturesque Roaring River originates in a 20,000,000 gallon (about 75,700,000

Bagnell Dam forms one of Missouri's most popular features, Lake of the Ozarks.

liters) spring, plunges over twin waterfalls and rushes through the hills with the terrific roar that provides its name.

Many of the state's rivers are fed by springs. In fact, probably no state surpasses Missouri in the number of large springs. Big Springs near Van Buren, is the largest single-outlet spring in the world, with a maximum daily flow of 846,000,000 gallons (about 3,202,000,000 liters) of sparkling, cold, clear water. Only the Snake River in the northwest is fed by more springs and a bigger volume of spring water than Missouri's Current River.

Altogether there are about 500 major springs in Missouri. Twenty-seven of these are mineral springs. The most noted of them are found in the Excelsior Springs region. The two ferro manganese springs there are the only ones of their type in the United States.

Most of the eight major lakes of Missouri are man-made. The best known of these is the fabled Lake of the Ozarks. Formed when Bagnell Dam was thrown across the Osage River near Bagnell, the main rivers and many tributaries were backed up into so many twisting valleys that the shape of the lake on the map looks like a writhing dragon with slashing tail, tossing head, and clutching talons.

Next in fame, and first of the large artificial lakes of Missouri is Lake Taneycomo, formed when the White River was dammed. Other lakes of the state include Pomme de Terre, Wappapello, Clearwater, and parts of Bull Shoals Lake, and Table Rock Lake.

CLIMATE

Missouri has less extremes of climate than some other regions in the humid continental area. Winters are comparatively mild, although occasionally in some parts there may be both very cold and surprisingly mild weather. The heel lies farther south than all of Virginia and some of North Carolina and Tennessee. Its climate is considerably more mild on the average than the rest of the state. Precipitation ranges from an average of about 50 inches (about 127 centimeters) in the southeast to 32 inches (about 80 centimeters) in the northwest.

16

Footsteps on the Land

BEFORE THE MEMORY OF MAN

Missouri was the scene of one of the earliest and most important of all discoveries of archaeology. Albrecht Kock was investigating the region on the Bourbeuse River when he found spear points in association with mastodon bones that proved mastodons and human beings lived here at the same time. This discovery, in 1838, was the first of its kind in the Americas and came only two years after the first such discovery was made in Europe.

No one was certain just when these people lived or how long human beings have lived in present-day Missouri. They were there at least 10,000 years ago and may have been there 20,000 or even 30,000 years ago.

The earliest occupants of Graham Cave (in present Montgomery County) were probably living there 10,000 years ago. They are called Early Man. Because of the importance of the stone tools and weapons found there, the region has been designated Graham Cave National Historic Landmark.

In several parts of Missouri, items have been found that belonged to people who lived there in prehistoric periods. After Early Man, these included Archaic Man, Woodland Man, and Mississippi Man.

The most startling fact about prehistoric times in Missouri is that a great civilization sprang up there about a thousand years ago. Even more astounding is that the center of this civilization was a great metropolitan community (called Old Village) on the site of present-day St. Louis. The metropolitan area occupied both sides of the Mississippi, just as is the case today. Strange, too, is the fact that a secondary metropolitan center of prehistoric culture sprang up where Kansas City is today.

People came from great distances to trade at these prehistoric centers on the great rivers. Game, ochre and other pigments, wood for bows, and salt were important items for barter. Salt was produced at salt springs not far from Old Village. Fine pottery was made and was much in demand. One typical piece was a jar with a cut design known as Ramey Incised. Pottery water bottles were shaped in the forms of fish and human heads. Bean pots, ladles, and jugs were skillfully made. Ochre was used for body coloring, for painting of pottery, and for designs on altars and walls.

Hair ornaments and pins were made of bone. Shells were turned into spoons, hoes, and scrapers. Jewelry was fashioned from a variety of materials. Tooled copper work was created with great skill. Some of the rarest prehistoric items found in Missouri are the Malden plates of copper, formed in the shape of eagles with human heads.

Woodworking tools were extremely sharp stones, and craftsmen cherished their razor-sharp adzes so much that many of these tools were buried with their owners.

Large hollowed-log dugout canoes made travel a comparatively simple matter throughout the whole Mississippi Valley area. Other objects found indicate that trade may have been carried on with peoples as far away as ancient Mexico. Open mines provided flint stones for knives, spear and arrowheads, and axes.

For some reason the Mississippi Valley civilizations had declined before Europeans reached the region. The Indians found there at that time were much more primitive. It is not known whether they were the descendants of the earlier people who had lost many of their skills or whether they were an entirely new group.

The most impressive remains of the earlier civilizations are the great mounds of earth the people raised for many purposes. Some of these were burial mounds; others were raised to hold temples and houses of chiefs, or for fortifications. The largest prehistoric mound in Missouri is the one near Caruthersville, 400 feet (about 122 meters) long, 35 feet (about 11 meters) high and 250 feet (about 76 meters) wide.

Eighteen hundred mounds have been noted in the Poplar Bluff region alone. A semicircular earthwork of the Hopewell people in Saline County is called the Old Fort. Some of these mounds were still used by the more modern Indians as burial places. Oval-shaped Blue Mound, near Horton, is the burial place of the well-known Chief White Hair of the Osage.

Ozark Bluff Dwellers, *a painting by Steve Miller.*

Many of the stone paintings and carvings found in Missouri (pictographs and petroglyphs) are thought to have been created by prehistoric artists, although many are also believed to have been made during historic times.

LAND OF THE MISSOURI AND OSAGE

Those Indian groups known to recorded history in Missouri were principally the Osage, to the west and south; the Missouri to the northwest; and some of the Ioway to the north and northeast.

Physically, the Osage were probably the most remarkable people of all the Indians found in America. Few of their men were under 6 feet (about 1.8 meters) tall, and many were over 7 feet (about 2.1 meters). Naturalist John James Audubon, who knew many Indians, called them "well-formed, athletic and robust men of noble aspect." According to another naturalist, "The activity and agility of the Osage is scarcely credible. They will not uncommonly walk from their villages to the trading houses, a distance of 60 miles (about 97 kilometers) in a day."

The Osage villages were built on high land or a terrace, with rectangular houses placed to form a circle. The chief's house, a larger structure, often was placed within the circle. Houses were at least 15 feet (about 4.6 meters) wide and from 35 to 100 feet (about 11 to 30 meters) long. During the hunting season the permanent villages were deserted except by those who were unable to hunt, and most of the people lived in temporary villages.

The women and children gathered edible foods, nuts, persimmons, and water-lily roots; they also cultivated crops—principally corn, beans, and squash or pumpkin. Before their activities began each day, the girls had the part in their hair painted red, representing the path of the sun as it crossed the day, giving them the hope of long life.

Osage people were familiar with simple science in such fields as astronomy and medicine. They made remarkable medicinal use of many roots, leaves, and tree barks. In spite of almost continuous warfare, they were noted for the care of their aged and invalids. Meat taken in a hunt was often shared with those who were not able to get their own.

Positions of leadership were generally hereditary, and power was concentrated in a few chiefs. However, there was at least a degree of democracy. The warriors were always consulted in tribal council before important decisions were made. Another notable fact about the Osage was that they remained unchanged and unharmed by the white man's ways probably to a greater degree than any other Indian group. Alcoholic drinks did not seem to hold the fatal fascination for the Osage that they did for others. Many had contempt for Europeans and their ways. Old Chief Hashakedatungar once remarked, "You are surrounded by slaves. Everything about you is in chains, and you are in chains yourselves. I fear if I should change my pursuit for yours, I too should become a slave."

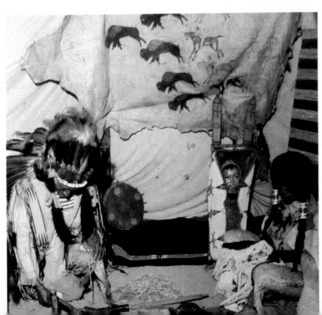

A diorama in St. Joseph Museum illustrating the life of the Indians.

DE SOTOS AND CADILLACS—GOOD FOR TOURING

Did Spanish explorer Hernando De Soto reach present-day Missouri? That question has puzzled historians for many years. It is known, of course, that he organized a great expedition of 600 men and explored much of southeastern United States. Missouri authority Leonard Hall says, "There were three chroniclers of the De Soto expedition, and by carefully sifting and matching up their accounts, historians have been able to trace his route with fair accuracy. . . . Since there is general agreement as to Indian tribes met and types of landscape traversed, there seems little reason to doubt that De Soto and his band . . . reached their 'farthest north' among the granitic knobs of the St. Francois Mountains in what is now Iron County."

This, of course, if accurate would make them the first Europeans to set foot in Missouri. Another great Spanish expedition, led by Francisco Vasquez de Coronado, was making its toilsome way overland from the west. There are historians who feel that Coronado reached as far east as Missouri and that De Soto and Coronado must have camped within a few days march of one another in July or August, 1541. There is no historical evidence to prove the accuracy of the interesting speculations about these early discoveries.

In the regions he did visit, De Soto killed and deposed many Indian leaders and did much to upset the Indian civilizations he found. He and his men also brought their diseases, and these were especially deadly to the Indian people because they had no chance to build up immunity over centuries as the Europeans had been able to do.

Parts of the region visited by De Soto were not seen by Europeans again for more than a hundred years. But the troubles he brought with him continued to plague the Indians of the whole vast southeast region and helped to bring about their rapid decline.

In 1673 the canoes of the party headed by Father Pierre Marquette and Louis Jolliet pushed down the Mississippi River from the north and made another of the many historic discoveries for which they were famous. They were first to see the mouth of the mighty

Missouri River. Written history of the region began with Marquette and Jolliet.

During the years immediately following, it is probable that French woodsmen, known as *couriers des bois,* became acquainted with present-day Missouri.

Nine years after Marquette and Jolliet, French explorer Robert Cavelier, Sieur de La Salle, passed the Missouri region on the Mississippi. When he had reached the mouth of that river, La Salle claimed the whole vast territory of the Mississippi Valley in the name of King Louis XIV of France. In King Louis' honor it came to be known as Louisiana.

French headquarters in Quebec were a tremendous distance by water and land travel from the Missouri country. Because of this, development by the French was slow. Before the century ended, however, French Jesuit missionaries visited the Missouri region to convert the Indians, and the first European settlement in Missouri was founded in 1700. This was St. Francis Xavier Mission. It is interesting to note that this mission is within the boundaries of present-day St. Louis. However, the mission was abandoned in 1703. By this time traders with the Indians and other explorers had investigated most of Missouri and had given names to many of its rivers and other features.

In 1712 the French gave a fifteen-year contract to monopolize the trade of Louisiana to Antoine Crozat. He had heard that there were rich silver lodes in Missouri and sent his representative Antoine de la Mothe Cadillac to find them. Cadillac was the famed founder of Detroit, Michigan, and the man whose name was used for the well-known automobile so many years later.

Cadillac dug for silver at Mine la Motte, also named in his honor, but he did not locate any rich silver strikes—only lead. In spite of this, the rumor grew in France that there were great riches in precious metals in the Louisiana country. A Royal Company of the Indies was set up in France, and many invested large sums of money in the hope of quick wealth. Mines were opened at Mine la Motte and at Mineral Fork of Big River. The company agent, Philip Renault, came to the Louisiana country in 1720 with fifty miners and some slaves. He expanded prospecting and mining in southeast Missouri but there apparently were no precious metals. The whole speculation, known as the Mississippi Bubble, burst.

More practical was the groundwork laid by Charles Claude Du Tisne, who visited the Osage Indians in 1719 and opened up trade with them. As early as 1714 Etienne de Bourgmond made his way up the Missouri River as far as the Platte River. He dealt very fairly with the Indians of the region, and they grew almost to worship him.

To protect the French claims against the English, De Bourgmond set up Fort D'Orleans on the Missouri River near the mouth of the Grand River in 1723. This was kept up until 1728, and was the earliest French effort to control the Missouri River region.

NEW BEGINNINGS AND NEW MASTERS

The French were well established on the Illinois side of the Mississippi in such villages as Kaskaskia, but until about 1735 there were no permanent European settlements in Missouri. At about that time some of the French residents of Kaskaskia moved across the Mississippi and made their home in what came to be called Ste. Genevieve—the first permanent settlement in Missouri. From here there was a growing trade with both Canada and New Orleans.

In 1762 Maxent, Laclède and Company began their monopoly of the fur trade between the Missouri and St. Peters rivers.

About the same time St. Louis was established in 1764, word came that in a secret treaty signed two years earlier France had ceded her territory of Louisiana west of the Mississippi to Spain. In 1765, the French Governor of Fort de Chartres surrendered Illinois to the British and moved to St. Louis, making this the capital of Spanish upper Louisiana. Spanish officials arrived in 1770.

Within five years Maxent, Laclède and Company was doing a business of $80,000 a year in furs, even though in 1765 their monopoly was taken away by the Spanish. Traders, merchants, outfitters, new settlers, especially from Illinois, moved into Missouri. As the fur trade increased, St. Louis became a remote center of culture.

23

Both the French and British had lived on the friendliest terms with the Indians. They recognized the Indian land claims and found no need for forts or other protection. However, when the American Revolution came, the Spanish fortified St. Louis and built blockhouses in many other parts of the territory.

Spanish officials took the side of the Americans and helped George Rogers Clark in his struggle with the British. In May, 1780, a force of about 1,000 Indians and 24 white traders attacked St. Louis. There were only 50 soldiers in St. Louis, but with the help of 250 people of the town, they withstood the attack. This kept the important Mississippi supply routes open for American troops in the west.

Other troubles came to the settlements in the form of ruthless river pirates. Then in 1788, the Year of the Ten Boats, ten boats and their crews made a systematic sweep up the river, driving the pirates out. St. Louis and other river towns grew rapidly after this. More than $200,000 in fur trading was carried on there each year.

Before long, the Spanish authorities became alarmed by the westward movement of American settlement. By opening or closing the port of New Orleans, Spain very nearly controlled the commerce and lives of western Americans. Many Americans moved into Spanish territory and became Spanish citizens, in order to be able to use the Mississippi freely. Spain had very liberal land policies. Land was granted free; there were no land taxes, and Americans without funds were given supplies and equipment. Because of this there was a growing number of Americans living on the west side of the Mississippi, including such names of later fame as Moses Austin.

In 1800 Napoleon forced Spain to return Louisiana to France. Spanish officials remained in charge, and in 1802 they closed the port of New Orleans to American trade. When American representatives protested this move, they were astounded to be given an offer to buy all of Louisiana, which, of course, was done.

On March 9, 1804, in a colorful ceremony at St. Louis, Captain Amos Stoddard formally received the upper Louisiana territory in the name of the United States. The region was placed under the control of the Territory of Indiana, William Henry Harrison, governor. In 1805 Congress created a separate territory of Louisiana.

On Monday, May 14, 1804, the expedition headed by Captain Meriwether Lewis and William Clark left St. Louis on what was to become the country's most famous journey of exploration. By this

A statue commemorating the signing of the Louisiana Purchase.

time, the first region of their trip up the lower Missouri was well known. As they toiled up the rapid river, all of those in the party who kept diaries wrote of the richness and beauty of the Missouri region.

On the second day out, Lewis almost met disaster. He slipped while climbing on a 300-foot (about 91 meters) bluff on the river bank, but fortunately caught himself after falling only 20 feet (about 6 meters). At the foot of that bluff the party marveled at the names of early travelers carved in the walls of a cave and at the picture stories of prehistoric men who had visited there. The cave was lost for many years, but was rediscovered in the early 1950s.

They reached the future location of Westport Landing and Kansas City on June 26. On June 29, one of the men, Hall, was given fifty lashes for stealing whiskey, another, Collins, a hundred lashes for being drunk on post and permitting Hall to steal the whiskey. The party celebrated the Fourth of July near present St. Joseph by firing one of their mounted swivel guns; an extra ration of whiskey was issued, and to close the celebration with an unplanned note, one of the men was bitten by a rattlesnake. They all were affected by the extreme mid-summer heat, and at the mouth of the Nodaway River, one of the men suffered sunstroke. They soon passed the borders of present-day Missouri and went on into history.

After their triumphant return, President Jefferson appointed his friend Meriwether Lewis the second governor of Louisiana Territory in 1807, replacing unpopular James Wilkinson, the first governor. After Lewis' death, his former partner, William Clark, was named governor. The Osage Indians made a treaty with the government to give up part of their land if the United States would assist them against the attacks of other Indians. To help in this, Governor Clark in 1808 established Fort Osage at present-day Kansas City—the first American outpost set up in Missouri.

SETTLING THE INDIANS

More and more Europeans flooded in, and trouble with the Indians grew. This was complicated by the fact that many eastern

26

Indians had moved to Missouri after being displaced from their ancestral homes. As early as 1784, 400 Shawnee under Chief Peter Cornstalk had begun a village near Old Appleton. Spain had granted lands to many displaced groups. Eastern Indians living in Missouri at one time or another included Delaware, Wea, Piankashaw, Kickapoo, Michigamea, and Cherokee. Both the native Indians and the newcomers feared the coming of the settlers would force them out, as it had done without fail in other areas.

From 1811 to 1815 Indian wars plagued Missouri. During the War of 1812, the British encouraged the Indians to fight Americans wherever they found them, and the frontier received almost no help from the government. Nevertheless, the settlers built their own forts and defended themselves valiantly.

Typical of their bravery was the unverified action of Mildred Cooper. When Fort Cooper was besieged by Indians, she volunteered to go for help. When her father asked her if there were anything she wanted, she replied, "Only a spur, Father." According to a local account, "Like the arrow from the bow, Milly and her good steed flew beyond the opened portals." When hours passed, her friends at Fort Cooper were sure she had been killed or captured. Suddenly a rescue party appeared, with Mildred at the head, and drove the Indians away.

In 1815 leaders of nineteen Indian groups met at Portage des Sioux with government representatives and signed treaties ending the war. Ten more groups did the same the following year. From that point on in Missouri, the story of the Indians was the same sad tale of rebuff and displacement, until in 1837 the last of the once proud and haughty owners of Missouri, the Osage, moved sadly to new lands in Kansas. Today there are no Indian reservations in Missouri.

A FAIR SHAKE

Indian wars were not the only troubles to plague the new territory during its early years under American rule. On December 16, 1811, at about two o'clock in the morning, settlers in the region of New

Thomas Hart Benton's mural, Pioneer Spirit, *can be seen in the Truman Memorial Library at Independence.*

Madrid were shaken from their beds. Houses creaked and groaned; the ground rose and fell in swells. Cracks formed in the land; rivers changed their courses; islands disappeared; lakes were formed. For almost two years hardly a day passed without a new tremor in a large area. The earthquakes of this period were the worst ever known in the region.

In 1812 Congress had created Missouri as a separate territory. When the Indian troubles were resolved, more new settlers flooded in.

It was an attractive region. One early traveler wrote of the Ozark region: "The country abounded in millions of deer, turkeys, bear, wolves, and small animals. I remember, as my father moved west, that we could see deer feeding in great herds on the hills like cattle, and wild turkeys were in abundance. Wild meat was so plentiful that early settlers subsisted on it. Bees abounded and were hunted for beeswax, while furs and hides served as currency of the country."

28

When a new family moved in, settlers helped them in their house raising. Trees were felled, timbers squared, and a small house could be put up in a day. Usually a house-warming dance was held the same night, with all celebrating their accomplishment. So many dancers crowded onto the floor of one house in St. Charles County that the floor they had just built gave way and dropped them into the cellar. They had to make it over again.

In the field of business, Auguste and Pierre Chouteau were the leading fur traders in the early period in the 1820s. Trader and explorer Manuel Lisa established the Missouri Fur Company. Even the great firm of John Jacob Astor could not compete with it as Lisa's men went from their St. Louis base to the farthest fur regions of the Rockies.

Steamboats made their appearance on the Mississippi, and in 1819 the steamboat *Western Engineer* became the first vessel of the inland navy of the United States and the first steamboat to navigate the Missouri River. It was designed to frighten and subdue the Indians, with a bow that looked like a serpent. From the gaping head of the serpent poured smoke and flames.

By 1818 the growth and development of the region was so great that Missouri asked Congress for permission to write a constitution in preparation for statehood. This caused a furor in Washington. Because of its large number of slaves, Missouri was expected to be a slave state, and there was great opposition in Congress to creating more slave states.

However, Maine was ready to be admitted as a free state. Those who supported Missouri said they would not admit a new free state unless Missouri was admitted as a slave state. After long debate and many changes, Congress finally agreed that both Maine and Missouri would be admitted, but that slavery would be prohibited north of 36 degrees and 30 minutes north latitude. This agreement in Congress is commonly known as the Missouri Compromise.

On August 10, 1821, President James Monroe proclaimed Missouri's admission as the second state to come from the Louisiana Territory. Alexander McNair was the first governor, and David Barton and Thomas Hart Benton were the first United States Senators.

The Madonna of the Trail, *a statue at Lexington depicting the pioneer mother of covered-wagon days, was dedicated by Harry Truman in 1928.*

Yesterday and Today

GOING AND COMING

In the period between statehood and the Civil War, Missouri became one of the world's greatest jumping-off places—a point of departure for an expanding America, The Gateway to the West! In 1822 William Bicknell left Franklin with a small group, and in a journey of great hardship opened the way to the Spanish town of Santa Fe, New Mexico. This Santa Fe Trail became the first principal road to the West, and its eastern end was always in Missouri, moving from Franklin to Independence and finally to Westport.

During the 1840s the rush of immigrants to the West began, and Missouri cities were the assembling points for the prairie schooners that rolled across the plains in ever increasing numbers. Steamers brought people and their supplies to St. Joseph, Westport, and other river towns. There the wagon trains were outfitted and began their weary trek over the various trails.

Hopeful thousands left the frontier comforts of Missouri for the almost unknown lands of the Oregon territory over the Oregon Trail. Others headed for California. As early as 1844 a wagon train of 800 people left the new village of St. Joseph for California. Among them was an immigrant named James W. Marshall. When the news came that Marshall had found gold in California, thousands of fortune hunters hurried to Missouri, anxious to find any kind of transportation to the hoped-for riches. Probably more wealth was gained by those who stayed in the state to supply the needs of the gold hunters than by those who made the ghastly trip.

St. Joseph "was packed so full of people that tents were pitched about the city and along the opposite bank of the river in such numbers that we seemed besieged by an army," Rudolph Kurz reported. In the three months from April to June, 1849, 1,500 wagons crossed the river there. In eight months of the same year, 123 permanent buildings were built at St. Joseph, 64 of them brick.

Not all who came to Missouri considered it only as a point of departure. In 1825 Missouri had the opportunity to honor one of

America's heroes. General Lafayette visited Missouri, and was entertained at a grand banquet and ball at St. Louis in Bennett's Mansion Hall. Another Missouri visitor, Charles Dickens, in 1842, made one of his few kind comments about America when he described St. Louis' Planters Hotel as "an excellent house, and the proprietors have most bountiful notions of providing the creature comforts."

Missouri was not so hospitable to another group. When Mormon leaders were driven from the east, they chose Missouri as a refuge. In 1831, Joseph Smith, leader of the Church of Jesus Christ of Latter-Day Saints, came to Independence and announced that this region had been revealed as a promised land for Mormons. Within a year more than 1,200 Mormons arrived in the Independence region. Their neighbors feared and distrusted them. Violence broke out and the Mormons were forced to leave for other parts of the state.

In 1836 the state legislature established Caldwell County as a Mormon refuge. The Mormons established Salem and Far West as new towns. Far West was laid out with magnificent proportions, a great temple in the center, and four main streets 100 feet (about 30 meters) wide. Far West grew to 4,000 in population within a year.

Mormons became so powerful and successful that their neighbors once again began to quarrel with them. Eighteen Mormons were massacred at Haun's Mill. Governor Boggs ordered them all to leave the state. General Samuel D. Lucas ordered General A. W. Doniphan to execute Mormon leaders who were sentenced to be shot. Indignantly, General Doniphan disobeyed: "It is cold-blooded murder. I will not obey your order. . . . " Most of the leaders finally escaped, and the last of the Mormons had left the state by 1839.

In a strange spirit of vindictiveness the buildings of Far West were torn down, and only a cornfield murmurs where this once prosperous community stood.

WARS AND RUMORS OF WARS

In another conflict, the war with Mexico in 1846, Missourians played a much more valiant and gallant part. The state furnished more troops than any other state for that war. The Army of the West was composed mostly of Missourians, and brave General Doniphan became a hero of the war.

One of the most famous trials in American history began in St. Louis in 1847. In the Old Court House there, a slave, Dred Scott, sued for his freedom. The case was appealed through various courts to the Supreme Court of the United States. There in 1857 Chief Justice Roger B. Taney gave the Court's famous decision. The Court declared that slaves could not sue in Federal Court. They were chattel of their masters and could never be citizens. The court said that the Missouri Compromise was unconstitutional and that Congress had no right to decide whether a territory should be free or slave. Dred Scott was given his freedom by his master in the year of the Supreme Court decision, and he lived one year in civil freedom before his death. The Dred Scott case helped increase the controversy over the slavery issue.

As the argument over slavery grew in intensity, it became increasingly clear that Missouri was terribly divided. The Kansas-Nebraska act of 1854 gave those two territories the right to decide for themselves whether or not they would permit slavery. It was apparent that Nebraska would be a free state, but Kansas was not certain. Slavery supporters in Missouri felt it was natural that Kansas would become a slave state. When they saw the efforts made by societies in New England to send free-state settlers to Missouri, many Missourians moved into Kansas Territory to establish land claims. They elected a legislature, later called illegal, that legalized slavery in Kansas.

Antislavery groups from the north responded to this threat by sending more groups of settlers to Kansas with money and support of powerful eastern leaders. Armed southerners rode the streets of Kansas City shouting "Death to all the damned Yankees." Open warfare came to the Kansas-Missouri border region, with both sides attacking the strong points of the others. Fighting was finally ended for the most part in 1858.

The border war violence made it appear that Missouri was a true slave state, but actually the majority of Missourians were not on either side. Most of the 115,000 slaves in Missouri were held in a relatively small area, particularly along the Missouri River, and their owners were in a minority. Most of the antislavery group were the foreign-born people of the state who lived in St. Louis, and in Franklin, St. Charles, and Gasconade counties.

Before war came, the average Missourian hoped for a compromise between the two sides. However, by 1861, when Claiborne F. Jackson was inaugurated as governor, opinions had begun to change. Jackson called a state convention to sound out the will of the people. Not one pro-slavery delegate was elected. The convention decided that there was no adequate cause to impel Missouri to dissolve her connection with the Federal Union.

A PECULIAR HORROR!

With the nation at war, Missouri was vital to both sides. Control of the Mississippi was tremendously important, as were the resources and manpower of the state. Governor Jackson was loyal to the South and did all he could to bring Missouri into the Confederacy. Leaders of the pro-Union forces were Francis P. Blair and Captain Nathaniel Lyon.

President Lincoln called for troops from the states, and Governor Jackson refused, but Blair offered his privately trained militia. Lyon armed them from the great arsenal at St. Louis, and sixty thousand muskets from the arsenal were secretly shipped to Illinois to prevent them from falling into Confederate hands. Camp Jackson was set up near St. Louis supposedly to train the state guard. However, Captain Lyon marched on the camp and captured it because he heard that its real purpose was to capture the St. Louis Arsenal. When sympathizers in the crowd resisted, shots were fired, and the war had begun in Missouri—a war that had, as one writer said, a peculiar horror all its own.

Lyon (now a general) occupied the state capital, Jefferson City, and went on to where the southern supporters had dug in near Boonville. The short, indecisive battle there was the first of the Civil War in Missouri. Confederate troops in Missouri grew in number. Union troops were beaten in the Battle of Wilson's Creek, near Springfield, where General Lyon was killed. After the victory of General Sterling "Old Pap" Price at Wilson's Creek, Price became the principal Confederate figure in Missouri.

Union forces lost another desperate battle when Colonel James A. Mulligan had to surrender at Lexington, and the entire garrison was taken prisoner. Although he had been deposed, Governor Jackson called the remnant of his legislature together at Neosho, and they

Dred Scott

declared Missouri to be a part of the Confederacy. As a result of this action, Missouri was officially admitted as the twelfth state of the Confederacy.

St. Louis served as the base for Union operations in the Midwest, but Southern troops controlled most of the rest of Missouri until the spring of 1862, when Northern troops began an offensive and drove them out of Missouri. Strong Confederate forces were able to unite below the border, and in the Battle of Pea Ridge, Arkansas, Northern forces were severely outnumbered. However, Union General S. R. Curtis cleverly and bravely won the battle, which is considered to have saved Missouri for the Union.

Among Union leaders who began their Civil War careers in Missouri was Ulysses Simpson Grant, who took part in the Missouri campaign. Legend tells of the Confederate soldier from the Ozarks who had General Grant in the sights of his rifle and failed to shoot. "I wasn't right certain it was Grant on that horse," he explained. "Hill people don't waste their lead on shots they can't call."

Organized war ceased for the time in Missouri, but a new and even worse guerrilla warfare took its place. Northern volunteers from Kansas looted, burned, and murdered with a free hand. Most Union leaders and their troops considered Missouri to be a Confederate state, and they treated the people harshly. Southern bands were organized for revenge.

According to the Civil War Centennial Commission of Missouri, "The number of participants engaged in guerrilla warfare was small, and battles were raids, skirmishes, and ambushes. Yet it took a terrific toll of life, and unlike the war fought by the armies, there was no respite, no rules, and no military objectives. . . . It was a war of terror, surprise, sabotage, and arson. . . . Their activity against the civil population created such fear and disorganization that society collapsed in some areas.

"The Confederate guerrilla forces . . . fought a total war, very personal in nature, cold-blooded, using unorthodox hit-and-run tactics. . . . They not only avenged many personal wrongs . . . but made a real contribution to the Confederate war effort in the West. For three years they kept Missouri embroiled in a private war, a partisan war fostered by an unfortunate political and military situation which might have been better handled by the Union authorities. The fierceness and fury of this war appalled all Missourians, and touched most of them personally."

The most notorious of all guerrillas headquartered in Missouri was William Clark Quantrill. The name Quantrill's Raiders is remembered while that of many Civil War groups is forgotten. "Bloody Bill" Anderson was one of the worst of Quantrill's men. He became a guerrilla leader for revenge of his father and two sisters, whose deaths he blamed on Federal forces. At times his cruelties were barbarous. At Centralia he captured a train carrying 23 unarmed Union soldiers, lined them up and massacred them. He himself was killed in an ambush in Ray County in late 1864 and buried in Richmond Cemetery. Cole Younger, who fought with Anderson, later formed a Wild West Show. When he came to Richmond and learned that Anderson had no funeral service, he hired a preacher and had his circus band play for services for his unlamented friend.

In late 1864, General Price once more invaded Missouri. At Fort Davidson, near Pilot Knob, 1,000 Union men held off 8,000 Confederates long enough to give St. Louis a chance to organize its defenses so Price did not dare to attack it. Battles were fought at Glasgow and Lexington. On October 23, almost 30,000 troops took part in the bloody Battle of Westport, sometimes called the Gettysburg of the West. Kansas City did not fall, and Price at last was pushed south below the border. The war was over in Missouri.

The incredible total of 1,100 battles and skirmishes had taken place in the state, amounting to 11 percent of all the engagements of the Civil War. A hundred and forty-nine thousand Missourians participated in the war—109,000 in northern armies and an estimated 40,000 in southern.

By a constitutional convention, Missouri's slaves were emancipated in 1864. Governor Thomas C. Fletcher proclaimed the slaves free on January 11, 1865, and Missouri became the first slave state to free its slaves. Because it remained loyal to the Union, Missouri escaped some of the awful trials of reconstruction that were suffered by other slave states.

MEET ME IN ST. LOUIS

St. Louis escaped damage in the Civil War and actually profited through the war. The huge sum of $180,000,000 was spent by the chief quartermaster for supplies of all kinds, and the city's industry soon grew to large proportions.

The first national convention ever held west of the Mississippi came to St. Louis in 1876. There the Democratic party nominated Samuel J. Tilden for President. The following year St. Louis government was separated from the county government with a charter that has been a model for other cities. In 1878 the first of the famed annual Veiled Prophets celebrations was held in St. Louis. The nation's second oldest symphony orchestra, the St. Louis Symphony, was founded in 1880.

Most Missourians quickly forgot their differences of the war, but for a long time after the war the whole Midwest was plagued by bandits, most of whom had been wartime guerrillas in Missouri. The most notorious of these were the James boys, former Quantrill raiders, who were born on their father's farm near Excelsior Springs. Jesse James was finally murdered in St. Joseph by former associates who wanted the $10,000 reward. The Younger brothers, the Bald

Thomas Hart Benton's mural shows Jesse James holding up a train.

Knobbers, Tom Turk, and Sam Hildebrand (who had 80 notches on his gun) were other desperadoes. Belle Starr, notorious woman outlaw, was born into the family of a Carthage hotel keeper. She later was shot in Texas. By 1882 most of the outlaws had been quelled.

Another troublesome matter came to a close in 1896 when the Supreme Court of the United States settled a border dispute carried on between Missouri and Iowa since 1839. This came to be known as the Honey War because the region included many of the bee-hive trees prized by early settlers for honey deposited in the hives in the hollow trunks.

A Missouri sheriff was arrested by Iowa authorities for trying to collect taxes in the disputed region. An Iowa court awarded a judgment against a Missouri man for having cut one of the bee-hive trees. Both governors sent troops into the area, and it looked as if real fighting might take place, but matters soon calmed down although the matter was not settled for almost sixty years.

In 1893 Kansas City attracted international attention when its brilliant fire department won an international competition in London under its leader George C. Hale. Leading cities of the world sent their fire fighting experts to learn the Kansas City methods.

In 1900 Kansas City again showed its spirit. The Democratic national convention was scheduled to be held in the city's wonderful new convention hall. On April 4 a fire completely leveled the hall, the city's pride. Before the flames were beaten back, the decision was made to rebuild within the three months before the convention. Crews worked seven days a week and around the clock, and tools were not put down until July 3. The new convention hall was ready when the Democrats were gaveled to order on the morning of July 4. William Jennings Bryan was chosen to run against President William McKinley.

World attention turned again to St. Louis in 1904, when the city played host to the American people in celebrating the hundredth anniversary of the Louisiana Purchase. The Louisiana Purchase Exposition was one of the greatest world's fairs ever held. Among other innovations, the ever-popular ice cream cone is said to have originated there.

When World War I turned the nations into armed camps, Missouri sent 140,257 into service with many under the Supreme Commander of the U.S. expeditionary force—Missouri's own John J. Pershing. Of the total, 11,172 died.

MODERN MISSOURI

After the war, one of the state's most pressing demands was to pull Missouri out of the mud. A $60,000,000 bond issue provided funds to build a fine road system. These roads provided the basis for the most significant economic changes in Missouri life since the Civil War. The numbers of automobiles, trucks, and buses began an increase that has not yet halted.

In World War II 450,000 Missouri men and women served in the armed services. The war was made more personal for Missouri through the leaders from the state who played prominent roles—especially General Omar M. Bradley and General James H. Doolittle. Even more important, however, as the war came to a close, was the man who was only a heartbeat from the Presidency and a native of Missouri. When President Franklin D. Roosevelt died on April 12, 1945, the first Missouri man to become President of the United States was Harry S. Truman.

An American fleet sailed into Tokyo harbor. When on September 2, 1945, the Japanese signed the surrender papers to end the war, the ceremony had a particular significance for the people of Missouri. Several rows of United States and other allied officers stood at attention on the deck of one of the country's mightiest battleships, the *Missouri*. On a simple table covered with a black cloth decorated in gold lay the large sheets of the surrender documents. Slowly the Japanese representative signed his name, while General Douglas MacArthur looked on with the others. Missourians were grateful that the deck of the great ship bearing the proud name of their state had been chosen as the site of the Japanese surrender. At anchor, the *Missouri* lay in the very heart of Japan as a symbol of the American soil and the American people it represented.

Turning with relief from the things of war, Missouri experienced both progress and problems in the decades that followed.

GATEWAY!

In 1966 the nation dedicated a monument in the form of an enormous stainless steel arch on the banks of the Mississippi River in St. Louis. This is an awe-inspiring symbol of Missouri's role in the past as the Gateway to the West. Even more important, it is hoped that this unique monument will always symbolize the state as a gateway to even greater progress in the future.

THE PEOPLE

Missouri can look back with satisfaction on the many ethnic backgrounds that have been combined to make her energetic people of today. The French were the earliest, and even today a French Creole dialect of the eighteenth century is spoken in a few areas.

Those of German origin have been especially significant. The first great wave of German immigration began at St. Charles in 1832. The 65,000 German residents of St. Louis were crucial in keeping Missouri in the Union during the Civil War.

Traces of medieval England still survive in some parts of the Ozarks, and other sections of the Ozarks are known as the Irish Wilderness. Belgians, Italians, and Scots have combined their efforts and abilities in the making of the state. The many who have come from neighboring states have had great effect—particularly the large numbers from Kentucky. Black progress has been notable, and black leaders have been especially distinguished in the field of music.

In late 1976 the people of the state mourned the untimely death of Congressman Jerry Litton, who was killed along with his family in a plane crash, shortly after he had received the Democratic nomination for Senator.

The Republican National Convention at Kansas City's Kemper Arena, in 1976, nominated President Gerald Ford for a second term.

Dogwood blossoms provide spring beauty.

Natural Treasures

TREES AND PLANTS

Missourians look with gratitude on their wealth of trees. The delicate tracery of redbud and the clustered blossoms of hawthorn, the state flower, brighten the spring. The crowning glory of the state tree, the dogwood, spreads its waxy blossoms across the spring countryside and dots the fall landscape with shining red fruit and leaves of crimson or purple.

The amazing variety of Missouri's trees includes bald cypress, pumpkin ash, corkwood, water locust, swamp cottonwood, bitter pecan, tupelo, overcup oak, black willow, honey locust, and pawpaw, as well as the more familiar elm, oak, hickory, and sycamore. Evergreens, such as the gnarled junipers, cling to Ozark rocks. One of America's rarest trees, the smoke tree, is found in Missouri, as well as the Osage orange, most prized of all woods for making archery bows.

Much of the forest cover of the state was cut away by unthinking logging practices, especially on the Ozark slopes. However, since 1931, in a brilliant program of reforestation, the state and the Federal government have bought up land for reforestation, and much of the woodland treasures of the state have been restored. A third of the state's land is in timber—with two-thirds of this being in the Ozark region.

Missouri prairies and woodlands are blessed with the amazing variety of 2,281 flowering plants. Possibly the most cherished are the rare purple fringed orchid and some other local orchids, tucked into out-of-the-way corners of the moist woods. Trilliums, larkspur, columbines, oxalis, violets, wild geranium, verbena, flame flower, blazing star, adder's tongue, cone flower, beardtongue, wild petunia, and phacelia are among the 1,250 kinds growing in the highlands.

The prairies were once covered with never ending stretches of many grasses. Prairie flowers still include many described by C.J. Latrobe in 1832: "God has here with a prodigal hand scattered the seeds of thousands of beautiful plants. . . . When the yellow suns of autumn incline over the west, their mild rays are greeted by the appearance of millions of yellow flowers which seem to clothe the undulating surface of the prairie with a cloth of gold." Prairie blossoms include anemone, meadow rose, turtlehead, white snakeroot, and river-bank grape.

Among the water plants are shining pondweed, American frogbit, and lady's eardrops.

John Hardeman's garden, established before 1840, near Old Franklin, is considered the first plant experiment station in the Mississippi Valley.

RUNNING, FLYING, CRAWLING

The large animals once so plentiful in Missouri are now found only in zoos. The last great herd of elk was gone by 1841, when at least 500 were killed by Indians; the last of the countless buffalo had disappeared by 1850. Squirrels and other small game, of course, are still plentiful—rabbits, skunks, western fox, opossum, muskrat, and raccoon, with some mink and red fox.

Wild turkey still can be found today in Missouri.

Four hundred species of non-game birds have been recorded in Missouri. Mockingbird, cardinal, purple finch, woodpecker, and blue jay are the most common. Baltimore oriole, indigo bunting, whippoorwill, and goldfinch are often seen. The little Carolina parakeets used to be so numerous that they made the sycamores look like Christmas trees. They have disappeared.

Notable among the birds of the Ozarks are the bald eagle and such exotic birds as the beautiful green herons often seen resting in willow thickets of the Ozarks, great blue herons, and American egrets.

Missouri streams and lakes are full of popular fish such as catfish and bass, and the state's hatcheries keep these well stocked.

Among Missouri's snakes, the rattlesnake is still to be found. However, times have changed since the days when 700 rattlesnakes were killed in one day in Clarksville.

MINERALS

Mineral resources of Missouri are among the richest in the Midwest. Carthage marble is world famous, and many other varieties of building stone are plentiful. Cement, lime, coal, barite, and, of course, lead are abundant. Refractory fire clays of Missouri have been important for generations. Iron-ore mines at Pea Ridge and Pilot Knob are considered tremendously important. Missouri's Vibornum Trend is now the world's richest lead producing district, yielding large amounts of zinc, copper, and silver, as well.

According to some experts, billions of gallons of petroleum, perhaps as much as the country's known reserves, may lie in oil bearing sand in an area of western Missouri from 12 to 20 miles (about 19 to 32 kilometers) wide and 85 to 90 miles (about 137 to 145 kilometers) long. Estimates of the potential oil reserves run to billions of barrels. Modern methods of steam and underground combustion may make it possible to tap this type of source, which could not be produced in the past.

People Use Their Treasures

INDUSTRIOUS MISSOURI

Missouri manufacturers produce more than nine billion dollars worth of goods each year.

In less than twenty-five years, McDonnell Douglas Aircraft of St. Louis has grown from two employees to over 35,000 to become the largest single private employer in the state. It made the famed Mercury and Gemini space capsules and is noted for its other space equipment. Another Missouri contribution to the space age is the Rocketdyne plant of North American Aviation at Neosho.

In a far different field of transportation equipment, Cape Girardeau is a leading center of towboat manufacturing. St. Louis is the leading shoe manufacturing center of the world, and the Kansas City area ranks first in the production of vending machines. Hallmark Cards, of Kansas City, is probably the best-known producer of greeting cards. Another Kansas City manufacturer, Burnson Instrument Company, was the first manufacturer in America to produce quality theodolites in quantity. (Instruments for measuring angles.)

Among the well-known breweries is the Anheuser-Busch Company of St. Louis. Monsanto Chemical Company, also headquartered at St. Louis, is another world leader in its field.

Pioneer Missouri manufacturers included Watkins Mill near Excelsior Springs, the first woolen mill west of the Allegheny Mountains, and the glassmakers of Crystal City. The Crystal City glass works came into being because almost limitless supplies of special quality glass sand were available there. When poet Walt Whitman visited Crystal City in 1879, he wrote, "What do you think I find manufactured out here and of a kind of clearest and largest, best, and most finished and luxurious in the world . . . ? Plate glass!"

One Missouri manufacturer, Earl Sawyer Sloan, operated a livery stable. He bottled his own liniment to relieve bruises and sprains of

Eagle jet fighters in production at the McDonnell Douglas Corporation.

horses. When he found the liniment was just as effective for humans, he went into the business of manufacturing on a large scale. Sloan's Liniment became a household word.

For more than fifty years, Missouri has been the country's leading state in lead production. Lead has been important in Missouri ever since Mine La Motte began production in 1715. Missouri ranks high in zinc production and is a major producer of copper and silver.

Potosi is the focus of the major center of barite production in the United States. A.P. Green Refractories Company of Mexico, Missouri, has almost a world monopoly on certain types of fire clay products. Gray marble from Carthage quarries has been used in famous buildings such as Macy's Department Store in New York and the Science and Industry and Field museums of Chicago.

Galena, a bluish-gray mineral, is one of the principal lead ores. Missouri is the world leader in lead production.

*The Missouri mule
is still a
famous symbol.*

Iron Mountain was once thought to be solid iron and at one time was a leading source of that mineral. Now the iron ore pellet production of Pilot Knob Pellet Company of Meramec Mining Company at the great Pea Ridge source has added to Missouri's mineral production.

Lead is the mineral bringing in the largest revenue to Missouri. Others are stone and zinc. The total mineral production in Missouri is valued at nearly a billion dollars.

AGRICULTURE

At one time the Missouri mule was probably the best-known product of the state's farms, before machinery took over his duties in the fields and in the armies of the world. Now cattle and grain are the most important sources of farm revenue, and livestock accounts for about 65 percent of Missouri's total receipts from agriculture. The state's agricultural income is well over $2,500,000,000.

Missouri's leading agricultural products are beef, pork, soybeans, corn, and dairy products. Other leading products are poultry and eggs, cotton and cottonseed, wheat grain sorghum, barley, tobacco, red clover seed, watermelons, potatoes, apples, Lespedeza seed, peaches, strawberries, and tomatoes.

Missouri leads the nation in the production of fescue seed and in pure-bred cattle herds.

Tobacco is a multi-million dollar crop, and many are surprised to learn that Weston has the largest loose-leaf tobacco market west of the Mississippi. The chant of the tobacco auctioneer is a familiar sound in warehouses there.

The Stark Nurseries at Louisiana, Missouri, established in 1816, are considered the oldest in the nation.

Missouri has long been noted for producing fine saddle horses. Audrain County is known widely as the saddle horse center of the world. Each spring and fall the community of Mexico is the scene of saddle horse auctions.

Almost from its earliest history the Missouri region has been a leader in the fur business. St. Louis still retains the unofficial title of world's largest raw fur market.

TRANSPORTATION AND COMMUNICATION

Missouri claims a number of firsts in communication and transportation: first Pony Express run (from St. Joseph, April 3, 1860); first international balloon race (St. Louis, 1907); first dirigible meet (St. Louis, 1908); first international aviation meet (St. Louis, 1910), set new speed record at 60 miles (about 97 kilometers) per hour and new endurance record of an hour and ten minutes, and cross-country record of 75 miles (about 121 kilometers); first newspaper west of the Mississippi (*Missouri Gazette,* St. Louis, 1808); and first broadcast of a midnight mass (Old Cathedral, St. Louis, 1922).

Its key position with relation to the three great rivers upon which most of the early travel and goods flowed—the Mississippi, Missouri, and Ohio—early made Missouri important in transportation. Today St. Louis is second only to Chicago as a center of United States transportation of all types—railroad, truck, bus, automobile, water, and air.

As early as 1789, the Spaniards had established a crude road, called El Camino Real (the King's Highway), from St. Louis to New

An oil painting by Charles Hargems shows the first Pony Express Rider leaving the stables on April 3, 1860.

Madrid. Another early road of importance was the Boone's Lick Trail, running from St. Louis to Franklin. It was part of a disconnected and rather unidentified transcontinental highway. Soon regular stagecoaches were running, and shortly an extension went as far west as Fort Osage. A stage driver of the 1840s wrote: "We did not always stick to the road. There were no fences. When one track became too muddy or rough with ruts, we drove out on the prairie or made a new road through the woods." Another traveler wrote, "If the mud does not quite get over your boot tops when you sit in the saddle, they call it a middling good road."

51

Along the pioneer trails trundled the clumsy covered wagons, often painted bright colors. Some travelers were able to afford carriages, while others could only walk, with packs on their backs holding all their worldly possessions. Inns sprang up along the roads, and where there were no inns, the travelers could generally count on the hospitality of even the poorest settlers.

Rivers, deep enough, provided water highways somewhat easier to travel than muddy roads. The *bateaux* of the early French settlers

Boat Race *by Currier & Ives*

were succeeded by the flatboat of later pioneer rivermen. Abraham Lincoln once floated past the Missouri shores, poling a flatboat to New Orleans.

The steamboat period was probably the most colorful in all American transportation. The elegant passenger boats, the puffing freight boats with stern or side paddles, and even the showboats, made the rivers busy and exciting. The Missouri River was extremely difficult to navigate. Some said that navigating the Missouri during low water was like putting a steamer on land and sending a boy ahead with a sprinkler. Skilled Missouri River pilots earned as much as $1,000 per month.

Exciting races often took place between some of the giant boats on the Mississippi. The best known of these was the race between the *Natchez* and the *Robert E. Lee*. The largest of the paddlewheelers was the enormous *J.M. White II*. Its side paddles alone were four stories high, and the smokestacks were 75 feet (about 23 meters) tall.

When the railroads came, steamboating began to decline. However in recent times, towboats snaking long strings of heavy barges have brought more traffic to the rivers than they ever knew before. The port of St. Louis now handles many millions of tons of freight per year. Congress voted in 1912 to improve the Missouri River channel. Almost constant improvement has been carried on ever since in both the Missouri and the Mississippi.

St. Louis was host in 1849 to about a thousand delegates to the first national railroad convention, where Thomas Hart Benton urged quick building of a transcontinental railroad. The first 5 miles (about 8 kilometers) of railroad in Missouri were opened in 1852 by the Pacific Railroad between St. Louis and Cheltenham. From that time on, railroads grew rapidly in the state. Jefferson City prepared to celebrate the arrival of its first train in 1855, but the celebration turned to tragedy when the trestle collapsed and twenty-eight were killed.

The world's first all steel railroad bridge, the Eads Bridge, was built over the Mississippi at St. Louis in 1878. The idea for the railway mail car originated at Hannibal and the first one was built there.

Today St. Louis is the nation's second largest rail hub.

Harry S. Truman's birthplace in Lamar.

Human Treasures

MR. PRESIDENT

On the evening of April 12, 1945, Vice-President Harry S. Truman took the oath of office as President of the United States, upon the death of President Roosevelt. A story is told that when President Roosevelt chose Mr. Truman to be his vice-president, someone in Washington said "Who is Harry Truman?"

Mr. Truman was not too well known to Americans and President Roosevelt had not kept him fully informed on many important matters of government. However, as one historian commented, "The crisp-speaking and sometimes jaunty Missourian was better prepared for what lay ahead than many of his contemporaries knew."

Born in Lamar in 1884, Mr. Truman served actively in World War I and later was a Missouri judge. His work in the United States Senate as head of a Congressional watchdog committee was so outstanding it won President Roosevelt's recommendation as his choice for vice-president in the 1944 election.

Before he became President, Mr. Truman was unfamiliar with the super-secret work on the atomic bomb. Suddenly he was faced with one of the major decisions of all times—whether or not to drop the bomb on Japan. When he finally decided to launch the atomic age with a roar of destruction, it was primarily because he hoped that the use of the bomb would make an invasion of Japan unnecessary and thereby save hundreds of thousands, perhaps millions, of lives. This it undoubtedly did.

Almost all predicted that Mr. Truman would lose the election of 1948. One of the leading Chicago newspapers even ran a huge headline claiming that the Republican candidate, Thomas E. Dewey, had won the election. This amused President Truman, who often commented about it. In this election Truman received 24,105,812 votes compared to 21,970,065 for Governor Dewey.

Not choosing to run in 1952, Mr. Truman retired to his beloved Missouri, where he worked tirelessly to write his memoirs and arrange his memorabilia in the Truman Library at Independence.

THE MARK OF TWAIN

A young boy slipped into his father's office to hide after he had played some prank on his family. Just settling down to go to sleep on the lounge, he watched a square of moonlight. As the light moved across the floor, it suddenly illuminated the dead body of a man lying there. The boy instantly decided to leave and took the window sash with him as he dived out head first. "It seemed more convenient at the time to do so," he explained later. As it turned out, the body was that of a stabbing victim who had been brought to the office for an inquest by the boy's father, who was then a judge.

The boy was Samuel Langhorne Clemens, who was later to gain world-wide fame as a writer. This experience and many others in his native Missouri formed the basis for many of his stories such as *Tom Sawyer* and *Huckleberry Finn.*

Sam Clemens was born in Florida, Missouri, and grew up in Hannibal. Many of his true experiences as a boy were woven into the stories of Tom and Huck. One of his boyhood friends, Tom Blankenship, was the original Huck Finn, Sam's partner in such events as that at Selm's store. Young Blankenship sold Selm a coon skin for ten cents. The clerk threw it on a pile of furs in the rear of the store. Sam climbed through the window, got the fur back, and Blankenship sold it again. They kept this up until the swindle was discovered.

Sam Clemens had a slight career as an author in the newspaper of his brother; he also served very briefly as a Confederate volunteer during the Civil War and became for a time a river pilot on the Mississippi. Later in far-off Nevada, Sam Clemens was trying to decide on a pen name to begin a new career in writing. He remembered how the river men would measure the depth of the river with a knotted rope and call "mark twain" as a certain depth was reached. He decided to take Mark Twain as his pen name. He became one of the truly creative writers in American history.

The Celebrated Jumping Frog of Calaveras County and Other Sketches appeared in 1867 and was the first of his works to gain wide recognition. He described his wanderings in the West in *Roughing It,* and told of his adventures on the river in *Life on the Mississippi.*

A mural by Thomas Hart Benton showing Huck Finn and Jim.

IN THE PUBLIC EYE

One of America's most respected military men was John Joseph Pershing. He was born near Laclede in 1860 and spent his boyhood there in a simple, ell-shaped, white frame house. He graduated from West Point in 1886 and took part in campaigns against the Apache Indians. He served in the Philippines during the Spanish-American War and led American troops hunting Pancho Villa in Mexico.

When America entered World War I in 1917, President Woodrow Wilson named Pershing as commander-in-chief of the American expeditionary force, where he achieved great success. He retired after the war. General Pershing is the only American ever given the rank of General of the Armies. This rank was originally created to honor George Washington, but there is no record to show that the appointment was ever made.

Alexander William Doniphan was in charge of unusual military maneuvers. During the Mexican War he organized the Missouri Mounted Volunteers, and led them on an overland march considered by many authorities as one of the most brilliant long marches ever made; the force, with no quartermaster, paymaster, commissary, uniforms, tents, or even military discipline, coverered 3,600 miles (about 5,800 kilometers) by land and 2,000 miles (about 3,200 kilometers) by water, all in the course of 12 months.

Thomas Hart Benton was one of the most distinguished public figures in Missouri history. For thirty years he served as one of Missouri's Senators and became one of the best known and most respected personalities in Washington. He was the leader in all matters in Congress promoting the expansion of the American West, and was the great friend of western settlers.

His life was one of those selected by Senator (later President) John F. Kennedy to be included in his book *Profiles in Courage*. This tells how Senator Benton, who opposed slavery, refused to support the pro-slavery people in Missouri although he knew it meant certain defeat for re-election. By this courageous act Senator Benton gave up his thirty-year career in the Senate. Even more important, it is possible that he may have given up a chance for the presidency, since his name frequently had been mentioned as a presidential possibility.

It is an interesting sidelight on Senator Benton's character that he was influential in the appointment of Mrs. Richard Gentry as postmistress of Columbia. She was one of the first women, if not the first, to receive an appointment of this type.

Other long Senate careers were those of two attorneys in the famous "Dog Trial" in the old courthouse at Warrensburg. A hunter, Charles Burden, sued the man who killed his noted hunting dog, Old Drum. The case was twice reversed and twice appealed. At the courthouse, Burden's attorney George G. Vest delivered his now famous oration *Eulogy to the Dog* and won the case. Vest later served in the Unites States Senate for twenty-four years. One of the opposing attorneys, Francis M. Cockrell, served in the Senate for thirty years, to equal Thomas Hart Benton's record.

James Beauchamp "Champ" Clark of Bowling Green served in the United States House of Representatives from 1893 till his death in 1921, except for one term, 1895-1897. For eight years he was Speaker of the House. In 1912 he was a candidate as Democratic nominee for President. He almost received the nomination, but last minute opposition by William Jennings Bryan threw the nomination to Woodrow Wilson. In the same year, Missouri's Herbert S. Hadley was seriously considered for the Republican nomination.

Besides Harry Truman, it may be said, at least in a technical sense, that Missouri had another "President" in the person of David Rice Atchison of Plattsburg. He was President pro tem of the Senate on March 4, 1849, when Zachary Taylor would have been inaugurated. However, this date fell on a Sunday and the ceremony was put off until the next day. Some authorities say that Atchison was in reality the President of the United States from the moment March 4 arrived until the oath was sworn the next day.

Enoch Herber Crowder of Edinburg, as judge advocate general of the Army, made sweeping changes and innovations in carrying out military justice. He devised a large and complex plan for creating a huge army for World War I; for this purpose his Selective Service Act was adopted by Congress.

CREATIVE MISSOURIANS

Joseph Pulitzer came to the United States from his native Hungary to serve in the Union Army during the Civil War. Next he worked as a reporter in St. Louis and then combined two St. Louis newspapers to form the *Post-Dispatch,* which he published. Later he also became a publisher of New York newspapers. His name lives on through the annual presentation of the famed Pulitzer Prizes, which he endowed to honor distinguished journalism, creative writing, and music.

One of the earliest intellectual weeklies—*Reedy's Mirror*—brought fame to its publisher, William Marion Reedy. He had great interest in the development of writers and thinkers throughout the nation, and many top writers first appeared in his publication.

Tom Bodine, of Paris, Missouri, was one of the few newspaper men to gain fame without leaving his home town. His editorial comments in a column called the *Scrap Bag* were often quoted throughout the country.

Other Missouri journalists included noted columnist O.O. McIntyre; Januarius Aloysius MacGahan, a correspondent whose name on an article would by itself attract attention; William Rockhill Nelson, whose Kansas City *Star* promoted civic improvements in his city; and Dale Carnegie; author of the popular book *How to Win Friends and Influence People.* Carnegie grew up in Pumpkin Center.

William Torrey Harris started an intellectual re-awakening known as the St. Louis Movement. He is credited with writing 479 books.

Novelist Harold Bell Wright began his literary career while he was pastor of the First Christian Church of Lebanon. His best-known work was *Shepherd of the Hills,* probably the most popular book associated with Missouri.

When Edgar Allen Poe read *George Balcombe* by Missouri novelist Nathaniel Beverley Tucker, he wrote of this work of an early period, "upon the whole the best American novel . . . its most distinguishing features are invention, vigor, almost audacity, of thought."

Another Missouri novelist, Winston Churchill, was born at St. Louis in 1871, and has been called the foremost novelist of his day. Some of his most popular works are *Richard Carvel, The Crisis,* and *The Crossing,* drawing strongly on the author's Missouri background.

Other noted Missouri authors include Rupert Hughes, born in Lancaster; Fannie Hurst, native of St. Louis; Homer Croy, of Marysville; Charles G. Finney, who wrote *The Circus of Dr. Lao;* John Breckenridge Ellis, author of *Little Fiddler of the Ozarks;* and John Montieth, whose *Parson Brooks* portrayed a Missouri hillman.

Beloved poet Eugene Field was born in St. Louis in 1850. One of his poems immortalized a familiar Missouri scene—*Lovers Lane, St. Joe.* Zoë Akins, poet and dramatist, born at Humansville, won the Pulitzer Prize in 1935 for her play *The Old Maid.*

One of the country's best known and most controversial artists is outspoken Thomas Hart Benton, grand-nephew and namesake of the Missouri Senator. John Rogers of Hannibal is a well-known sculptor. Cartoonist George McManus, born in St. Louis, created the long-popular comic strip about Maggie and Jiggs.

The man who probably gave the world more entertainment than

any other with his artistic endeavors spent his boyhood in Marceline. At the age of ten he drew cartoons with tar on his grandfather's barn door. He later advanced in cartooning, to create such characters as Mickey and Minnie Mouse and Donald Duck. His many movies, Disneyland, and Disney World have made the name Walt Disney a household word.

One of the most famous composers in the popular field was W.C. Handy, creator of *St. Louis Blues.* Tom Turpin added to the city's publicity with his *St. Louis Rag.* Composer Egbert Van Alstyne of Hannibal was the creator of *Memories* and *In the Shade of the Old Apple Tree.*

TYCOONS

One of the country's best-known merchants is J.C. Penney, born on a farm near Breckenridge. Mr. Penney founded one of the world's largest merchandising organizations. He became especially known for the stress he placed on fair practices in business. The J.C. Penney Missouri Farms near Breckenridge are noted for the modern system in which horses are raised.

Eberhard Anheuser and Adolphus Busch purchased a bankrupt St. Louis brewery. They developed a method of brewing beer without requiring pasteurization and pioneered in bottling beer. By 1900 the brewery they founded was the largest in the world. The Busch family remains prominent in St. Louis, owning among other properties the St. Louis Cardinals.

Busch Stadium, home of the St. Louis Cardinals.

George Hearst, mining tycoon, and father of millionaire publisher William Randolph Hearst, was born in Sullivan. The earliest of Missouri's industrialists was Moses Austin, who came to Missouri and improved lead mining and smelting processes after 1798. In 1818 he suffered reverses and went bankrupt. Austin died just after he had received permission to put into operation his plan for creating American settlements in Texas. This was done soon afterward by his son Stephen, who grew up in Missouri.

Early in life, Joyce C. Hall became interested in a new custom, the sending of greeting cards at Christmas and Valentine's Day. He could foresee that in the future millions of such cards would be sold for every occasion, particularly for birthdays. He established his Hallmark Company at Kansas City, and the company is still the leader in the greeting card field. Each year they produce different designs for cards, gift wrappings, party supplies, entertainment specialties, playing cards, and stationery. Mr. Hall also pioneered in sponsorship of quality television shows, and in great Kansas City building programs.

SUCH INTERESTING PEOPLE

Just before 1800, the Spanish government received a request for a land grant from an elderly man, and they quickly gave him 845 acres (about 340 hectares) in Missouri. So it was that famed frontiersman and pathfinder Daniel Boone once again took to the trail and arrived in St. Charles County, Missouri. He had been heavily in debt in Kentucky and he could not get title to his lands there, so at the age of 65 he went west to start life again.

The Spanish government gave this distinguished pioneer high honors. They added 8,450 acres (about 3,400 hectares) of land to his grant and made him a syndic (judge) of the region. This placed him in almost complete charge of the area. When the United States took over, again his land titles were in doubt. Finally a special act of Congress gave him title to the original 845 acres (about 340 hectares). His Kentucky creditors swept in and most of this land went to pay his debts. To keep up payment on his debts, the old man set out in his great canoe and trapped for furs on the streams of the Missouri River watershed.

Many of his family settled in the region and he loved to visit with them. Artist Chester Harding visited Boone at his cabin near Matson to paint his portrait. He asked the eagle-eyed old scout if he had ever become lost, and the answer was, "I was never lost, but I was bewildered once for three days."

When Daniel Boone died in 1820 he was buried in Bryan-Boone

Two portraits of frontiersman Daniel Boone; the one on the left by John James Audubon and the one below by Chester Harding.

Cemetery, but the bodies of Boone and his wife were later taken back to Kentucky, although Boone had said he would rather have his head on the block than ever go to Kentucky again. Several local ministers and missionaries tried to bring Daniel Boone into their folds. He told one of these, John M. Peck, "I always loved God ever since I could recollect," and there he let the matter drop.

A pathfinder of another age, Charles Augustus Lindbergh, received his greatest help and encouragement in Missouri. His pioneering solo flight across the Atlantic was financed by a group of St. Louis businessmen, and his plane immortalized "The Spirit of St. Louis."

One of the country's best guides and scouts was Kit Carson, who ran away from his home at Old Franklin in 1826 to begin a career that was to help in the expansion of his country from sea to sea. Another keen-eyed Western explorer was the famed scout James Bridger, who knew almost every foot of the Rockies.

One of the most notable black scientists was a Missouri native. George Washington Carver was born near Diamond in Newton County. He left Missouri early in his life. While he might have earned a great fortune with his brilliant agricultural discoveries—might even have been a successful artist—he preferred to devote his extraordinary abilities to the welfare of the black people through his work at Tuskegee Institute.

Also dedicated to her fellow man was Mother Rose Philippi Duchesne. When Mother Duchesne and four sisters of the newly founded Society of the Sacred Heart moved to Florissant, she wrote, "There was a moment this month when I had in my pocket only six sous and a half, and debts besides." From this small beginning, Mother Duchesne went on to become one of the best-loved women of the state.

Carrie Nation, crusader against liquor, is buried at Belton. During the years she lived in Missouri she had not yet begun her anti-saloon campaign. She taught in the schools at Holden, and was discharged for one of the most unusual reasons on record. She and her employers quarreled over the pronunciation of the letter "a."

Another Missouri woman of considerable notoriety was Martha

Canary, born in Princeton. She later became one of the most experienced frontier experts and was given the name of "Calamity Jane." Also fighting for her rights, but in a different way, was Mrs. Annie Baxter. She was elected clerk of Jasper County, but was kept from the post because it was said women could not hold office. She carried the case to the Missouri Supreme Court and won, attracting much favorable attention for her devotion to the rights of women.

Daniel Ralls must also be mentioned for his devotion. As a representative in the legislature, he was a strong supporter of Thomas Hart Benton. Ralls was seriously ill when the legislature was preparing to vote on Benton's first term as a United States Senator. When it appeared that Benton might be defeated, Ralls had himself carried to the assembly hall on a stretcher. "If I should faint," he ordered, "recover me there, and by no means take me out before I have given my vote." Benton was elected, and Ralls died in his home not long afterward.

Dr. William G. Eliot, of St. Louis, organized the Western Sanitary Commission, which provided medical service of unusual quality to care for the wounded in the Civil War. Dr. John Sappington of Arrow Rock was a pioneer in use of quinine for malaria, also an internationally recognized authority on fever treatments.

Missouri owes its "Boot Heel" to John Hardeman Walker. When Walker learned that the area in which he lived—south of the thirty-sixth parallel between the Mississippi and the St. Francis rivers—was not to be included in Missouri, he began a campaign to have the area made a part of the state. Because he was successful in this, Missouri now possesses its valuable southern extension.

Indian leaders of Missouri include Chief White Hair of the Osage, who went to Washington to plead that a Christian mission should be established among his people; Peter Cornstalk, eloquent Shawnee Chief; and his son, Chief Nerupeneshequah.

Westminster College, Fulton, was the site of Winston Churchill's famous "Iron Curtain" speech. To honor the occasion and Churchill's leadership, a twelfth-century London church, rebuilt by Christopher Wren in the 1600s, was rebuilt stone by stone at Fulton. The building now houses the college chapel and a Churchill Museum.

Teaching and Learning

Missouri has the distinction of establishing the first state university west of the Mississippi River as well as the first state university in what once was the Louisiana Purchase. The Missouri General Assembly provided that the university would be established in the county providing the greatest financial inducements.

People anxious to have the university in their towns made pledges of astonishing amounts. Some sold their houses, and others pledged more than they had. A commission decided that Boone County was the winner with $117,900 in pledges. The cornerstone of the first university building was laid in Columbia in 1840, and classes began in 1841.

The university has been a pioneer in many fields, most notably, perhaps, in journalism. In 1908 the university opened the first school of journalism in the world to grant a degree. As the years have passed, the school of journalism has continued to be recognized as one of the leaders in its field.

One of the most significant developments at the University of Missouri has been the establishment of a University Research Park Area. The heart of this Research Park is a 10-megawatt nuclear research reactor—the most powerful research reactor on any university campus in the United States. The branch of the university at Kansas City, formerly the University of Kansas City, also is noted for its work in science.

Another branch of the University of Missouri opened at Rolla in 1871 and is now one of the outstanding institutions of technology. The United States Bureau of Mines Experiment Station, United States Forest Service, United States Geological Survey, and Missouri State Geological Survey maintain headquarters on the campus.

St. Louis University, a Catholic institution, founded in 1818 as an academy, is the oldest university west of the Mississippi. It arrived at university status in 1832. Another notable university of St. Louis is Washington University. Its medical school is usually ranked among the top five in the country. Washington has developed its Research

The Harry S. Truman Library in Independence.

Center, located on a 2,000 acre (about 800 hectares) tract 20 miles (about 32 kilometers) from St. Louis. Research in medicine, space science, nuclear physics, genetics, geophysics, meteorology, soil erosion, air and water pollution, and many other fields may make this the leading research complex of the Midwest.

Lincoln University, Jefferson City; Central Missouri State University, Warrensburg; Southwest Missouri State University, Springfield; Northeast Missouri State College, Kirksville; Southeast Missouri State University, Cape Girardeau; and Northwest Missouri State University, Maryville, are other publicly supported institutions.

Stephens College, Columbia, is one of the country's noted colleges. Once a junior college, it now offers a limited number of bachelor degrees. Lindenwood College at St. Charles is one of the oldest colleges for women in the Mississippi Valley. Rockhurst College, Kansas City, is a four-year college of liberal arts, science, and business conducted by the Jesuits.

Saint Marys-of-the-Barrens, Perryville, founded in 1818, is considered Missouri's oldest institution of higher learning. William Jewell College was established at Liberty in 1822. Tarkio College developed when Tarkio built a county courthouse and then the county seat was established elsewhere. The unused building was transformed into a Presbyterian college.

Park College, Kansas City, is a self-help college where students can earn their way by working in one of the school's various business activities.

St. Stanislaus Seminary, Florissant, is said to be the oldest existing Jesuit Novitiate in the world. In 1824 St. Stanislaus school opened a school for Indian boys, the first of its kind in the United States.

Kemper Military School at Boonville is considered to be the oldest boys' school and military academy west of the Mississippi. School of the Ozarks near Hollister is an institution offering self-help opportunity at the college level.

A view of the Gateway Arch and the city of St. Louis from the Mississippi River. The arch was built as a reminder of St. Louis' historic position as the gateway to the West.

Enchantment of Missouri

CITY OF THE SAINTED KING

One of the most striking structures in the world stands on the banks of the Mississippi in St. Louis. This is the nation's tallest monument—a rainbow-shaped arch soaring into the sky with its outer face covered entirely by gleaming stainless steel. This is the Gateway Arch designed by architect Eero Saarinen; it is a reminder of the city's historic position as gateway to the west. However, it also stands for the modern spirit of St. Louis. It is the proud symbol of civic progress that is virtually remaking St. Louis. The work includes a complete rebuilding of 10 percent of the city at the cost of billions of dollars.

The heart of the new St. Louis is the Jefferson National Expansion Memorial, on the original site of old St. Louis, where the Gateway Arch now stands. This memorial is a $30,000,000 project financed jointly by the national and city governments. Two historic St. Louis buildings are preserved here. The Old Courthouse, where the Dred Scott case first came to trial, where Senator Benton delivered his famous oration "Westward the Course of Empire," and where U.S. Grant freed his only slave is located here.

Also preserved nearby is the old cathedral, begun in 1831. Now called Church of St. Louis of France, it is still an active parish. When the cathedral bell was cast, 200 Spanish silver dollars were melted into it to sweeten its tone.

The Visitors' Center at the park is placed underground so that the sweeping vistas will not be interrupted. Here is the Museum of Westward Expansion. An elevated central mall and parkway join the Jefferson Memorial and the Civic Center.

Next door to the Jefferson Memorial another ambitious building project has created the Busch Sports Stadium, the home of the St. Louis Cardinals, a $90,000,000 center patterned after the Coliseum of Rome. The 55,000 seat stadium features four parking garages accommodating 7,400 automobiles, a 400 unit motel, and office and commercial space.

Slum clearance, modern housing projects, and vast business development are all helping to shape the new St. Louis. A critical part of the new development was the plan created by the city to rid itself of the smog that was choking it. This plan was so successful that it was tried with equal success by Pittsburgh and other smog-bound cities.

The new city is in the tradition of the old—settled in 1764 and incorporated in 1808. One of the worst disasters to strike the city was the terrible fire of 1849 that spread from a steamboat and destroyed fifteen blocks in the heart of the town at the same time that a severe cholera epidemic was causing great anguish, suffering, and death. But the city soon bounced back from these twin plagues. Another difficulty occurred when the course of the Mississippi changed and threatened to leave the port of St. Louis lifeless behind a sandbank. The trouble was corrected by the army under the direction of a then little-known young officer—Robert E. Lee.

The city's early attention to cultural matters continues. The St. Louis Art Museum dominates Art Hill. As early as 1907 the people of St. Louis voted to support their art museum by a tax, a very unusual public action. It was originally the art building of the Louisiana Purchase Exposition of 1904.

The museum of the Missouri Historical Society in Forest Park's Jefferson Memorial building contains a fascinating river room, costume room, a selection of Lindbergh trophies, and other exhibits. The Museum of Science and Natural History features animated displays operated by the visitor, explaining all aspects of science. McDonnell Planetarium, opened in 1963, is one of the most advanced of its type and is housed in a particularly striking building.

The planetarium is found in 1,400 acre (about 567 hectares) Forest Park, the second largest city park in the country. St. Louis' oustanding zoo is also in Forest Park. The zoo is especially noted for the training of many of its animals and for public exhibitions of trained chimps and other talented zoo residents. The Jewel Box in Forest Park is an outstanding conservatory.

A building called the world's most advanced conservatory is the Climatron in Shaw's Garden, in the heart of the city. This unique

72

Left: The Climatron Botonical Gardens. Right: The St. Louis Art Museum. Both of these sites attract tourists to St. Louis.

structure is housed in a geodesic dome. The botanical gardens were given to the city by Henry Shaw. Among the unusual plants from all over the world are the artillery plants, which shoot their seeds from pods. The herbarium at the Botanical Gardens is one of the largest in the Western Hemisphere.

The St. Louis Sacred Music Society and the St. Louis Brass Band prepared the way for the St. Louis Symphony. The people of the city take great pride that they support the second oldest symphony in the country.

St. Louis Municipal Opera presents summer opera in Forest Park in the country's largest outdoor theater, which seats 15,000. The last of the old-time showboats, the *Goldenrod,* still presents old-fashioned entertainment on the river. A newer pleasure boat is the enormous excursion boat *Admiral.* This floating carnival accommodates 4,000 passengers; 2,000 dancers at one time can use the vast ballroom which extends almost the full 375 foot (about 114 meters) length of the boat.

73

The new St. Louis Cathedral is one of the largest churches in the country. It has beautiful mosaics and fine Byzantine architecture.

Lambert-St. Louis Municipal Airport is one of the country's largest. The growth of air transport in St. Louis already requires great expansion of the Lambert facilities and a vast new airport.

One of the nation's best-known celebrations is the annual Veiled Prophet Parade and Ball, which opens St. Louis' social season. A small group of St. Louis businessmen started the event to give the city an annual festival. Membership is kept a strict secret and the organization makes every effort to keep the identity of the Prophet a secret. A Queen of Love and Beauty reigns over the formal ball, which is preceded by an elaborate parade.

Another famed processional of a different type in the St. Louis area is the Corpus Christi procession at Florissant. The solemn ceremonial has been carried on with few interruptions since 1814.

HISTORIC SOUTHEAST

A number of picturesque customs are still followed in Missouri's oldest permanent settlement—Sainte Genevieve, founded 1735. On New Year's Eve in the ceremony of La Guignolee, revelers in masks troop from house to house. With them goes a fiddler to accompany the ancient French song they sing. In the United States only New Orleans preserved more of the old French Creole buildings than are found in Ste. Genevieve.

Another historic river town, New Madrid, hoped to be a New World utopia with no taxes, where worshippers flocked to churches of every creed. Wide streets were laid out. As the river changed and earthquakes came, the town was forced to move, and the first site of New Madrid is now under water near the Kentucky shore of the Mississippi. Even some recent residents, such as Mrs. Laura Hunter, recall, "All the buildings on the river were kept on rollers during my girlhood. Their owners kept rolling them back."

In the early days residents of New Madrid were bothered by the coming of a strange group called the Fanatical Pilgrims, who never

74

washed, never worked, or buried their dead, and were apt to burst into almost any house shouting "Praise God!" or "Repent!"

A museum of Sikeston displays what is said to be the world's largest collection of restored nickelodeons. Altenburg is one of the centers of German tradition. Belief in witchcraft and spells used to be common. One man told the tale that a local witch who had no horse turned him into a horse and rode him to a party. His biggest complaint was that she had left him tied in a plum thicket.

Cape Girardeau is the educational and commercial center of southeastern Missouri. Nearby is Trail of Tears State Park, commemorating the forced march of the Cherokee Indians and the route they took to Oklahoma. Near Jackson, Bethel Church was established, the first Baptist church west of the Mississippi.

At Keener Cave near Greenville there is a prehistoric wooden canoe almost perfectly preserved in the clear waters of a small lake in the cave. Montauk State Park is a charming small mountain retreat, surrounding Montauk Springs, the headwaters of picturesque Current River. Nearby Texas County, larger than Rhode Island, is the largest county in Missouri, with Houston as its appropriately named county seat.

Elephant Rocks are a group of strangely formed boulders of fantastic size near Graniteville. St. Michael's Catholic Church, an interesting building, was built under the direction of Father Lewis Tucker, who ordered a scriptural quotation carved in marble to be placed above the door: "My house shall be called a house of prayer." However, the carver went on with the end of the quotation, which reads, "but you have made it a den of thieves." Even though the undesired words were filled in with putty, they have been visible as a warning to any who might have such intention. Visitors to Millstream Gardens near Fredericktown are taken around in a covered wagon.

One of the finest exhibits of minerals anywhere is that of the Mineral Museum of the University at Rolla. The basic collection of the museum came from the display at the St. Louis world's fair of 1904. Another mineral attraction of Missouri is the natural tunnel near St. James. This is a passageway 150 feet (about 46 meters) long and 30 feet (about 9 meters) wide through a rock bluff. A spring in the middle of the passageway sends its waters out of both entrances.

Potosi is the site of the home and tomb of Moses Austin, whose plans brought the first American settlement to Texas. Another of Missouri's twenty-five caverns open to the public is Meramec Cavern near Stanton. Its first room is large enough to park 300 cars and house a dance floor. Visitors ascend up into the cave, not down.

Selma Hall near Crystal City is considered by some to be the finest ante-bellum home in Missouri. The first Protestant sermon in Missouri was preached in 1798 from a rock in the Mississippi at Herculaneum. Missouri Botanical Gardens Arboretum near Pacific preserves a typical example of Ozark landscape. Plants shown at the botanical gardens in St. Louis are raised there, and the orchid collection is said to be one of the largest in the world. The national Museum of Transport near Kirkwood is a showcase of transportation history. Exhibits include over thirty locomotives.

LAND OF THE HILLS—SOUTHWEST

One of the most unspoiled mountain areas of the country is found in the Ozarks of southwestern Missouri. Growing in popularity are the float trips, which take visitors drifting lazily down the many mountain rivers—fishing or just dreaming. The Ozarks are thought to have taken their name from the French phrase meaning territory of the Arkansas Indians, "aux Arkansas." This came to be *auxarks,* and finally in the English version—Ozarks.

Mountain crafts are popular in the region, and the Festival of Ozark Crafts is held each year at Silver Dollar City near Branson.

Making brooms in Silver Dollar City.

The work of the Ozark Basket Weavers group and other craftsmen may be purchased at many places along the roads. Marvel Cave near Branson has a 175 foot (about 53 meters) high mountain inside. The Lake Taneycomo area is a popular recreation spot, with headquarters at Rockaway Beach. Nearby Hollister was planned as a model village, taking advantage of the natural beauty. Commercial buildings were built of the half-timbered construction, making them look like an English village.

Mountain Grove is the site of the Missouri State Fruit Experiment Station which has won more than twelve international exposition medals for its work in the development of new fruit varieties.

Near Springfield is the Wilson Creek Battlefield National Park, dedicated in 1961 in memory of the bloody battle there during the Civil War. The Springfield National Cemetery is the only one where graves of Federal and Confederate soldiers are buried in the same cemetery. The Union and Confederate sections were separated by a fence. A bill was passed by Congress for an opening in this fence, and a gate was dedicated with formal ceremonies joining the two groups in death as they had not been in life. Two colleges and an art museum are other attractions of Springfield.

George Washington Carver National Monument at Diamond commemorates the birthplace of the noted black scientist. One of the main attractions is the winsome statue of the young Carver in the park. Another well-remembered birthplace is that of Harry S. Truman at Lamar. The modest white frame home where Mr. Truman was born is now preserved as a tribute to the 33rd President.

Liberal was founded by G.H. Walker as a community for free thinkers, a haven for those opposed to all religion. Later Walker became interested in spiritualism, and seances were held until a fire exposed them as fakes.

Lake of the Ozarks State Park is the largest in the state. Warsaw is the tourist center for the enormous lake, one of the country's most popular resort and fishing regions. Hanging Hollow near Warsaw is named for an execution that never happened. A young man convicted of murder stood under a tree in the hollow with a rope about his neck. Just before the deputies could complete their job, a messenger rode in madly to say they had the wrong man. The real murderer had just confessed elsewhere.

The bluffs of Devils Elbow near Hooker are named on many lists as one of the seven beauty spots of Missouri.

GREATER KANSAS CITY

Kansas City had its beginnings in a trading post in 1821. Its neighbors, Independence and Westport, came into being and prospered earlier. Kansas City was first known as Westport Landing and then as Kansas Town. It was incorporated in 1855 as the City of Kansas. As C.L. Edson wrote in a ballad, "They planted Kansas City, and the darn thing grew."

In the 1850s a New York reporter gave this description of the Kansas City river front: "A confused picture of immense piles of freight, horse, ox and mule teams receiving merchandise from the steamers, scores of immigrant wagons, and a busy crowd of whites, Indians, half-breeds, Negroes and Mexicans . . . much stir and vitality and the population, numbering two thousand, had unbounded, unquestioning faith that there was *the* City of the Future."

Urged on by such strong promoters of Kansas City as William Rockhill Nelson, the people of the metropolis have never wavered in that faith in their city. Nelson kept up a relentless agitation for civic improvement. Through his newspaper, the Kansas City *Star,* he constantly encouraged the citizens to realize his ideal of a city as beautiful as it was prosperous.

George Kessler, engineer, architect, landscape-gardener, worked to transform the once drab Kansas City almost completely. As Robert S. Townsend wrote, "If the founding fathers of that little settlement on the bend of the Missouri could only see her now! The French writer Maurois called our town one of the most beautiful cities in the whole world."

As a further contribution to the beauty of his city, Nelson was the principal donor of the William Rockhill Nelson Gallery of Art, one of the country's best. It is particularly well known for its Indian and

Indian Scout *by C.E. Dallin surveys modern Kansas City.*

Chinese art and for collections that range from modern back to the art of Sumeria of 3,000 years ago.

A commanding feature of Kansas City is its dramatic 300 foot (about 91 meters) high Liberty Memorial surmounted by a glowing flame. The Memorial was dedicated in 1926 by President Calvin Coolidge before the largest audience ever addressed by a President of the United States up until that time. There are memorial buildings at either side of the shaft, and one of these is the national shrine of the Rainbow Division of World War I and II. A lengthy and spacious mall leads up to the memorial. In 1961, the structures were rededicated as a "Memorial to International Understanding." At that time one of the world's five largest carillons, gift of Mr. and Mrs. Joyce C. Hall, was also dedicated. A daily concert of the carillon's 305 bells now serenades the city. Truman Sports Center and Crown Center are recent dramatic developments.

79

Nichols Fountain in Kansas City's Country Club Plaza, called the world's first shopping center.

Kansas City Museum features displays of the region's history, natural history, and anthropology. The natural history dioramas are especially interesting. A planetarium is also operated in connection with the museum. The great Kansas City Municipal Auditorium faces a landscaped plaza under which there is a large underground garage.

Swope Park of 1,756 acres (about 711 hectares) is home of the renowned Kansas City zoo. In Penn Valley Park is the Pioneer Mother Monument. This bronze group depicts a pioneer woman with her baby in her arms; she rides one of two plodding horses as the father and a guide walk beside her. It was the gift of Howard Vanderslice as a memorial to his mother and the mother of his wife. Swope Park is also the scene of outdoor musical plays given in the Starlight Theater for ten weeks during the summer.

The highly regarded Kansas City Philharmonic Orchestra was founded in 1933, and the city's Youth Symphony is also widely acclaimed.

One of the finest livestock shows in the country is the annual American Royal Livestock and Horse Show held in the Kemper Arena every October. Summer sees attention turn to the city's major league baseball team.

As home of President Harry S. Truman, the Kansas City suburb of Independence gained considerable fame, which has continued with the location of the Harry S. Truman Library there. This was built and furnished from donations, without cost to the government, and dedicated in 1957. For 166 years there was no systematic provision for preserving presidential papers. Now libraries have been set up for all recent Presidents. As President Truman wrote, "The papers of the Presidents are among the most valuable source materials for history. They ought to be preserved and they ought to be used." For this purpose the Truman Library has made available nearly 10,000,000 documents.

The museum features a mural by Thomas Hart Benton titled *Independence and the Opening of the West.* The former President's office is reproduced in exact detail. Colorful gifts contributed to the President from all over the world are displayed. An exhibit designed by Mr. Truman carries out his desire to make the presidential office more clearly understood by explaining what he called the six jobs of a President. Famous documents include the rough draft of the Fair Deal message, articles of the Potsdam Conference, and others. There is an exhibit of originals of cartoons given to Mr. Truman by the artists who drew them.

Perhaps the most moving exhibit is the original instrument of surrender signed by the Japanese in 1945 on board the battleship *Missouri.* A selection of the battleship's silver service is also displayed in the museum.

The Kansas City region is an unusual center of religious activity. The World Headquarters of the Reorganized Church of Jesus Christ of Latter Day Saints occupies impressive buildings in Independence, including a 7,000 seat auditorium. The World Headquarters of the Unity School of Christianity is also maintained at Independence, and the International Headquarters of the Church of the Nazarene is at Kansas City.

Historic old Fort Osage, first American fortification in the Loui-

Fort Osage has been reconstructed.

siana Territory, has been partially restored. Jim Bridger, pioneer of the West, is buried in Mount Washington Cemetery at Independence. Near Independence is Lone Jack Battlefield and Soldiers' Cemetery. A museum there contains dioramas and exhibits of the Civil War in Jackson County.

Another nearby city, Excelsior Springs, was noted as one of the country's leading health resorts. It is said to have the longest mineral water bar in the world.

Another nearby town is interesting for its name. A real estate agent was showing land to an eastern group. When they came over a hill one of the ladies exclaimed, "That's peculiar! It is the very place I saw in a vision in Connecticut." When they bought the land and laid out the town they named it Peculiar.

NORTHWEST

Battle of Lexington state historic site commemorates one of the largest battles of the Western Campaign in the Civil War. Anderson House, the center of the battle, has been restored. In 1852, Lexington was the scene of one of the worst accidents in river history when the steamer *Saluda* blew up, killing 250 people, mostly Mormons. At Lexington is one of the several Pioneer Mother Monuments erected in various states on the old National Road.

The annual Missouri State Fair is held in Sedalia. At Boonville, Thespian Hall, the first legitimate theater in Missouri, is still being used. Near Boonville is the grave of William Henry Ashley, founder of a pioneer trapping company, western explorer, lieutenant governor, and Congressman from Missouri.

Pershing State Park honors the memory of one of Missouri's most distinguished military men—General John J. Pershing. The park, near Laclede, Pershing's birthplace, preserves an extensive tract of virgin prairie grass, one of the few such grass tracts remaining in the country.

Memories are numerous in St. Joseph of the city's eminence as an assembly point for so many of the pioneers who journeyed to the

82

The St. Joseph Museum.

west. The Pony Express Stables have been rebuilt as a museum, and many western mementoes are on display at the St. Joseph Museum. The Jesse James House is open to the public. The home was supposed to be that of a quiet-living Mr. Howard, who was killed there and then was discovered to be the famous outlaw.

St. Joseph was known in the 1890s as being the wealthiest city per capita in the United States. The city is especially admired today for its unique 28-mile (about 45 kilometers) long boulevard system which brings the scenic countryside into the heart of the city.

NORTHEAST

Columbia has been an educational center from its earliest years. Of special interest on the 1,200 acre (about 486 hectares) campus of the University of Missouri are the General Library, largest between the Mississippi and the West Coast, and the university museums. One of these specializes in the subject of journalism, for which the university is famous.

The State Historical Society of Missouri is the state's official historical agency and with 15,000 members is the largest in the nation. It occupies the ground floor of the University of Missouri Library. Its reference library of 350,000 volumes is the third largest of its type, and its state newspaper library is the largest. The society also has in its art gallery the major collection of paintings by George Caleb Bingham in the United States.

A number of settlements on the Missouri River are particularly noteworthy for their German background. Hermann is known for its annual Maifest when traditional German costumes and customs add color to the festivity. Another community of German background is Dutzow. The settlers included many aristocratic and professional men who brought a rich background of German culture. St. Charles, founded in 1780, was the first settlement on the Missouri River. It became the state capital in 1821. Between 1832 and 1870 a wave of German settlers also came there. St. Charles County still boasts of many fine houses of distinctive German architecture.

The region around Defiance holds many memories of Daniel Boone and his family. The Nathan Boone house, home of Daniel's youngest son, is at Defiance. In the house the seven finely carved mantels with sunburst details are supposed to have been carved by Daniel Boone. And Daniel Boone is supposed to have held court, as a Spanish judge, under the giant judgment elm nearby. Mr. and Mrs. Boone were buried at Manthasville before their bodies were returned to Kentucky.

Bethel was founded in 1845 by Dr. William Keil, a German mystic who brought 500 of his followers to the new town, designed as a communal religious settlement. Dr. Keil's word was final in all matters. The settlement prospered and was known particularly for its manufacture of fine gloves. Fearing that outsiders settling nearby would contaminate his group, Dr. Keil made plans to remove the colony to Oregon. Keil's son, William, had planned to lead the first group to Oregon but he died before the trip began. His father had the body placed in an iron casket filled with alcohol so that his son could make the promised journey.

Mark Twain State Park at Florida was the first land in Missouri obtained by public subscription. The park contains the birthplace of the famous Missouri writer. The Twain boyhood home at Hannibal has been preserved and a museum there has many mementoes and local relics. The home has been restored and refurnished. The home of Laura Hawkins, who became Becky Thatcher in the author's writings, is also open to visitors. Life-size statues of Tom Sawyer and Huckleberry Finn are placed at the foot of the hill in Hannibal where the children played.

Twain himself described the Hannibal he knew: ". . . a Negro drayman, famous for his quick eye and prodigious voice, lifts up the cry, 's-t-e-a-m-b-o-a-t a-comin!' and the scene changes! The town drunkard stirs, the clerks wake up, a furious clatter of drays follows, every house and store pours out a human contribution, and all in a twinkling the dead town is alive and moving. Drays, carts, men, boys, all go hurrying . . . to a common center, the wharf. Assembled there, the people fasten their eyes upon the coming boat as upon a wonder they are seeing for the first time."

The home of Daniel Boone near Defiance.

MR. JEFFERSON'S CITY—THE CAPITAL

In 1821 the Missouri General Assembly assigned a commission to establish a new capital city on the Missouri River within 40 miles (about 64 kilometers) of the mouth of the Osage. When they selected the so-called city of Jefferson, it consisted of a tavern, mission, and foundry with a nearby river landing. When the General Assembly moved there in 1826, there were still only thirty-one families in the town. Today Jefferson City is the attractive, modern capital of Missouri.

Dominating the community is the great capitol building—the third capitol building in Jefferson City, the other two being destroyed by fire. The present imposing structure was finished in 1917 at a total cost of $4,125,000. In order to provide a firm enough foundation, 285 concrete piers were poured, each resting on bed rock. On these a structure 437 feet (about 133 meters) long and 200 feet (about 61 meters) wide was raised to a height reaching 262 feet (about 80 meters) at the peak.

The Capitol in Jefferson City.

The exterior of the building is pure white Carthage, Missouri, stone. An unusual feature of the construction is the number of columns—134 altogether—requiring a fourth of all the stone used in the building. At the entrance, the ponderous bronze front door, 13 by 18 feet (about 4.0 by 5.5 meters), is reputedly the largest since Roman times. The great carved relief on the river side of the capitol shows the signing of the treaty bringing Louisiana Territory to the United States. The outside grand stairway is 120 feet (about 37 meters) wide; on either side of it bronze figures represent the Mississippi and Missouri rivers. A heroic bronze statue of Thomas Jefferson stands on a marble pedestal in the center of the stairway. The interior stairway is more than 65 feet (about 20 meters) wide, said to be the widest inside stairway in the world.

Both chambers of the General Assembly are enhanced by superb stained glass windows. The lantern at the top of the dome is surmounted by a statue of Ceres, goddess of grain, sculptured by Sherry Fry. The once controversial murals by Thomas Hart Benton decorate the extreme west wing. Also in the capitol is the Missouri Resources Museum.

The executive mansion, home of the governor, is located where the first capitol building was built in Jefferson City. The present mansion was built in 1871. The winding stairway to the second floor is one of the finest in the state of Missouri. Of particular interest to visitors are portraits of all Missouri first ladies since statehood.

Missouri State Penitentiary and the National Cemetery are also found in Jefferson City.

"SHOW ME"

In summarizing the merits of his state, the average Missourian is quick to agree with an immigrants' guide of 1804 which eulogized, "There is no part of the western country that holds out greater attractions. . . ." The people of Missouri are glad of the opportunity when a visitor takes up the famous Missouri slogan and says, "Show me."

Handy Reference Section

Instant Facts

Became the 24th state, August 10, 1821

Capital—Jefferson City, settled 1823

State motto—*Salus Populi Suprema Lex Esto* (The Welfare of the People
        Shall Be the Supreme Law)

Nickname—The Show Me State

State bird—Eastern Bluebird

State tree—Dogwood

State flower—Hawthorn

State rock—Mozarkite

State mineral—Galena

State song—*Missouri Waltz,* melody by John Valentine Eppel, lyrics by
        J.R. Shannon, arranged by Frederick Logan

Area—69,680 square miles (180,470 square kilometers), including water
      area of 548 square miles (1,419 square kilometers)

Rank in area—19th

Greatest length (north to south)—300 miles (483 kilometers)

Greatest width (east to west)—280 miles (451 kilometers)

Highest point—1,772 feet (540 meters), Tom Sauk Mountain

Lowest point—220 feet (67 meters), near Cardwell

Geographic center—Miller, 20 miles (32 kilometers) southwest of
        Jefferson City

Number of Counties—114

Population—5,070,000 (1980 projection)

Rank in population—11th

Population density—72.7 persons per square mile (28 persons per square
        kilometer), 1980 projection

Rank in density—27th

Population center—In the Osage River, on the Osage County-Cole
        County Line, 8.7 miles (14 kilometers) southeast of
        Jefferson City

Birthrate—14.5 per 1,000 people

Infant mortality rate—18.5 per 1,000 births

Physicians per 100,000—139

Principal cities—

St. Louis	622,236
Kansas City	507,330
Springfield	120,096
Independence	111,630
St. Joseph	72,691
Florissant	65,908

You Have a Date with History

1541—Hernando De Soto may have reached Missouri
1673—Marquette and Jolliet discover Missouri River
1682—La Salle claims Mississippi Valley in name of France
1715—Cadillac opens Mine la Motte
1719—Du Tisne begins trade with Indians
1723—De Bourgmond establishes Fort d'Orleans
1735—Sainte Genevieve begun
1764—St. Louis established
1770—Spanish authorities formally take control
1800—Spain returns Louisiana to France
1803—United States buys Louisiana Territory
1804—Lewis and Clark journey through Missouri
1811—Indian wars begin
1821—Statehood
1838—"Mormon War"
1843—First great emigration to West embarks from Missouri
1846—Missouri contributes most troops to Mexican War
1856—Guerrilla warfare over Kansas question
1861—First land battle of Civil War (Boonville)
1864—Battle of Westport
1874—Eads Bridge Opened over Mississippi
1880—St.Louis Symphony formed
1904—Louisiana Purchase Exposition, St. Louis
1917—World War I; 140,257 Missourians in service
1921—Centennial of statehood celebration
1931—Bagnell Dam completed, forms Lake of the Ozarks
1941—World War II; 450,000 Missourians serve
1945—Missouri's first President, Harry S. Truman, takes office
1966—Gateway Arch dedicated, St. Louis
1976—Republicans nominate Gerald R. Ford at Kansas City Convention

Annual Events

February—Creative Arts Conference, Springfield
March—N.A.I.A. Basketball Tournament, Kansas City
May—Maifest, Hermann
May—Apple Blossom Festival, St. Joseph
May—Rodeo, Springfield
June—Feast of Corpus Christi Procession, Florissant, and Sainte Genevieve
July—Rodeo, Neosho
August—Missouri State Fair, Sedalia
September—Cotton Carnival, Sikeston
September—Bootheel Rodeo, Sikeston
September—4-H Interstate Show, St. Joseph
October—Veiled Prophet Parade and Ball, St. Louis
October—American Royal Livestock and Horse Show, Kansas City

Thinkers, Doers, Fighters

People of renown who have been associated with Missouri

Anheuser, Eberhard
Atchison, David Rice
Benton, Thomas Hart (statesman)
Benton, Thomas Hart (artist)
Bodine, Tom
Boone, Daniel
Bradley, Omar M.
Busch, Adolphus
Cadillac, Antoine de la Mothe
Canary, Martha (Calamity Jane)
Carson, Kit
Carver, George Washington
Churchill, Winston (novelist)
Clark, James Beauchamp (Champ)
Clark, William
Clemens, Samuel Langhorne (Mark Twain)
Cockrell, Francis M.
Crowder, Enock Herbert
Croy, Homer
Disney, Walt
Doniphan, A.W.
Doolittle, James H.
Duchesne, Rose Philippi
Field, Eugene

Finney, Charles G.
Hall, Joyce
Handy, W.C.
Hearst, George
Hughes, Rupert
Hurst, Fannie
Kinney, Joseph
Lewis, Meriwether
Lindbergh, Charles Augustus
McManus, George
Nelson, William Rockhill
Penney, J.C.
Pershing, John Joseph
Pulitzer, Joseph
Reedy, Marion
Sappington, John
Sloan, Earl Sawyer
Stark, Lloyd C.
Truman, Harry S.
Tucker, Nathaniel Beverley
Vest, George G.
White Hair (Chief)
Wright, Harold Bell

Governors of the State of Missouri

Alexander McNair, 1820-1824
Frederick Bates, 1824-181825
Abraham J. Williams, 1825-1826
John Miller, 1826-1832
Daniel Dunklin, 1832-1836
Lilburn W. Boggs, 1836-1840
Thomas Reynolds, 1840-1844
Meredith M. Marmaduke, 1844
John C. Edwards, 1844-1848
Austin A. King, 1848-1853
Sterling Price, 1853-1857
Trusten Polk, 1857
Hancock Lee Jackson, 1857
Robert M. Stewart, 1857-1861
Claiborne F. Jackson, 1861
Hamilton R. Gamble, 1861-1864
Willard P. Hall, 1864-1865
Thomas C. Fletcher, 1865-1869
Joseph W. McClurg, 1869-1871
Benjamin Gratz Brown, 1871-1873
Silas Woodson, 1873-1875
Charles H. Hardin, 1875-1877
John S. Phelps, 1877-1881
Thomas T. Crittenden, 1881-1885

John S. Marmaduke, 1885-1887
Albert P. Morehouse, 1887-1889
David R. Francis, 1889-1893
William J. Stone, 1893-1897
Lon V. Stephens, 1897-1901
Alexander M. Dockery, 1901-1905
Joseph W. Folk, 1905-1909
Herbert S. Hadley, 1909-1913
Elliott W. Major, 1913-1917
Frederick D. Gardner, 1917-1921
Arthur M. Hyde, 1921-1925
Sam A. Baker, 1925-1929
Henry S. Caulfield, 1929-1933
Guy B. Park, 1933-1937
Lloyd C. Stark, 1937-1941
Forrest C. Donnell, 1941-1945
Phil M. Donnelly, 1945-1949
Forrest Smith, 1949-1953
Phil M. Donnelly, 1953-1957
James T. Blair, Jr., 1957-1961
John M. Dalton, 1961-1964
Warren E. Hearnes, 1965-1973
Christopher S. Bond, 1973-1977
Joseph P. Teasdale, 1977-

Index

92

93

PICTURE CREDITS

ABOUT THE AUTHOR

With the publication of his first book for school use when he was twenty, **Allan Carpenter** began a career as an author that has spanned more than 135 books. After teaching in the public schools of Des Moines, Mr. Carpenter began his career as an educational publisher at the age of twenty-one when he founded the magazine *Teachers Digest.* In the field of educational periodicals, he was responsible for many innovations. During his many years in publishing, he has perfected a highly organized approach to handling large volumes of factual material: after extensive traveling and having collected all possible materials, he systematically reviews and organizes everything. From his apartment high in Chicago's John Hancock Building, Allan recalls, "My collection and assimilation of materials on the states and countries began before the publication of my first book." Allan is the founder of Carpenter Publishing House and of Infordata International, Inc., publishers of *Issues in Education* and *Index to U. S. Government Periodicals.* When he is not writing or traveling, his principal avocation is music. He has been the principal bassist of many symphonies, and he managed the country's leading non-professional symphony for twenty-five years.